From Entry-Level Employee to Group CEO:
Leadership Lessons from *The Three Kingdoms* and Admiral Yi Sun-sin

Jung Sung-ouk, CEO, is a central executive who leads Utop Construction and the Utop Group, playing a vital role in the growth and development of the group. Under his leadership, Utop Construction has consistently delivered stable results in the construction industry, successfully completing various construction projects both domestically and internationally. CEO Jung has emphasized implementing strategic management for the company's growth and presenting a forward-looking corporate vision.

1. Management Philosophy

CEO Jung operates the company based on leadership that emphasizes responsible management and innovation. He prioritizes customer satisfaction and values quality and safety, forming a management philosophy that has positioned Utop Construction as a trusted company in various fields, including construction, civil engineering, housing, and renewable energy. Furthermore, he strives for sustainable construction that is mindful of the environment by proactively adopting eco-friendly technologies and innovative construction methods to keep up with future construction trends. Through these efforts, he aims to enhance the company's long-term competitiveness and grow Utop Construction into a socially responsible enterprise.

2. Leadership and Achievements

CEO Jung has played a crucial role in strengthening the company's foundation and building a base for long-term growth. Notably, he has further solidified the company's standing by successfully executing large-scale projects. Under his leadership, Utop Construction has achieved sustained growth through a stable financial structure and efficient organizational management. He also works to enhance collaboration across various divisions within the group, maximizing synergies between affiliated companies. These efforts improve the competitiveness of the entire Utop Group, enabling it to maintain a solid business

3. Social Contribution and Corporate Responsibility
CEO Jung places a high priority on corporate social responsibility (CSR) and actively promotes various activities that contribute to the local community. For instance, Utop Construction engages in a wide range of social contribution activities aimed at supporting the community, strengthening its role as a company that coexists with local residents. Such initiatives also positively impact the company's credibility.

4. Future Strategy
CEO Jung is actively focused on adopting digital innovation and smart construction technologies to keep pace with changes in the future construction market. His leadership reflects a long-term vision that looks at both the present and future of Utop Construction, which supports the company's ongoing sustainable growth.

Contents

Preface : The Value of Leadership Across Generations
Part 1 : The Beginning of Leadership - Vision and Direction
    Chapter 1: Fundamentals of Leadership
    Chapter 2: Vision and Goals
    Chapter 3: Precise Decision-Making
Part 2 : Organizational Management - The Power of Talent and Communication
    Chapter 1: The Importance of Talent
    Chapter 2: Trust and Communication
Part 3 : Crisis and Challenge - The Tests and Triumphs of Leadership
    Chapter 1: Overcoming Crises
    Chapter 2: Decision-Making and Responsibility
Part 4 : Success and Failure - The True Value of Leadership
    Chapter 1: Learning from Failure
    Chapter 2: Humble Leadership
Part 5 : Preparing for the Future - Innovation and Sustainability
    Chapter 1: Flexible Leadership
    Chapter 2: Future-Oriented Management
    Chapter 3: The Attitude of a Future-Prepared Leader
Trend Forecasting and Innovation
Part 6 : Path to Sustainable Growth and New Challenges

Preface: The Timeless Value of Leadership

The Power of Leadership Across Generations

Leadership goes beyond simply managing and operating an organization. True leadership transcends time and place, moving people's hearts and guiding them toward a common goal. The stories of *The Three Kingdoms* and Admiral Yi Sun-sin may come from ancient wars and history, but the core values of leadership within them remain relevant today. Though these figures are historical, the challenges and hardships they faced are not so different from the complex management environments that modern leaders navigate every day.

Lessons in Leadership from *The Three Kingdoms* and Admiral Yi Sun-sin

The Three Kingdoms illustrates how numerous rulers and generals applied strategies and tactics, demonstrating the impact of their leadership on organizations and society. Figures like Liu Bei, Sun Quan, and Zhuge Liang not only maintained power through force but also led their organizations with personal charisma, strategic thinking, and decisive action in times of crisis. Although each had distinct personalities and leadership styles, they all succeeded in uniting people and preserving their organizations—an endeavor closely related to challenges faced by today's CEOs and management teams.

Today's business environment is more complex and competitive than ever. Market uncertainties, rapid technological advancements, and the diverse demands of stakeholders present challenges that require leaders to exercise flexible and strategic leadership. The essence of leadership demonstrated by the rulers of *The Three Kingdoms* continues to offer valuable lessons. Amid political instability, internal dissent, and external threats, they sought ways to protect and grow their organizations, with their choices profoundly shaping the course of history.

Liu Bei's Leadership - Vision and Talent Management

Liu Bei presented a compelling vision for unifying *The Three Kingdoms* and compensated for his own weaknesses by recruiting the brilliant strategist Zhuge Liang. His leadership underscores the importance for modern executives of setting long-term goals and identifying exceptional talent to address their own limitations. Although Liu Bei faced numerous failures, his persistence and decisiveness ultimately led his organization to success. This resilience exemplifies the value of a leader's unwavering commitment to the vision despite setbacks.

Sun Quan's Leadership - Flexibility and Agility

Sun Quan guided his organization through a flexible leadership style, adapting strategies according to circumstances. Sometimes he formed alliances with enemies, while at other times, he expanded his power through warfare. Sun

Quan's leadership illustrates how modern companies should respond agilely to rapidly changing market conditions. Recognizing the limitations of his own power, Sun Quan leveraged external alliances to protect and grow his organization. Today's executives similarly need a clear understanding of their strengths and weaknesses and should seek external partnerships to secure sustainable success when needed.

**Zhuge Liang's Leadership –
Strategic Thinking and Decisive Judgment**

Zhuge Liang, known for his strategic thinking and wisdom, led through calculated decision-making, even in times of crisis. He achieved victory against Cao Cao's massive army at the Battle of Red Cliffs and continued to protect his ruler with astute strategies. Zhuge Liang's leadership reminds modern leaders of the importance of cool-headed analysis and strategic foresight. Rather than being driven by short-term gains, today's executives must plan for the long-term future of their organizations, making decisions with clarity and precision to ensure enduring success.

General Yi Sun-sin's Leadership: Morality and Responsibility

General Yi Sun-sin exemplifies the moral and responsible leadership expected of those who lead an organization. In battles under extreme conditions, such as the Battle of Myeongnyang, he not only employed brilliant military strategies but also demonstrated a commitment to sacrificing everything to protect his organization. General Yi's unwavering dedication to his country and people reflects the essence of a true leader willing to put the organization's welfare before his own. His leadership emphasizes why modern executives must lead their organizations with high ethical standards. His deep trust and sense of responsibility toward his soldiers and officers inspired absolute loyalty and confidence in him. Similarly, today's leaders need ethical leadership and a commitment to build trust within their organizations, as these qualities are essential for long-term success. General Yi inspired his troops with a powerful vision and steadfast decisiveness, taking full responsibility as a leader until the very end.

Executives should follow his example by making responsible decisions that serve the organization's long-term interests, even in times of crisis, without compromising moral standards. General Yi Sun-sin's dedication reminds leaders that prioritizing the organization's well-being over personal gain is essential. In today's corporate world, responsible leadership fosters stability and trust, which, in turn, encourages members to dedicate themselves to the organization's goals.

Connecting the Leadership of Historical Figures with Modern Executives

The stories of the rulers from *The Three Kingdoms* and General Yi Sun-sin go beyond historical anecdotes; they offer powerful lessons for modern leaders. Faced with military crises and political conflicts, these leaders continually sought ways to protect and grow their organizations, adapting to changing environments. This book translates their stories into actionable strategies tailored to today's management landscape, providing insights on how modern leaders can make better decisions and guide their organizations toward success.

Leadership is the ability to move people beyond the limits of time and circumstance. The decisiveness, strategic thinking, and ethical leadership shown by the heroes of *The Three Kingdoms* and General Yi Sun-sin offer valuable insights for today's business leaders. Through their lives and leadership, this book provides practical advice and strategies to help modern executives navigate the diverse challenges they face and lead their organizations to success.

Today's executives are not just managers but creators of organizational vision, guiding and motivating people. Through this book, readers can learn from the leadership lessons of *The Three Kingdoms* and General Yi Sun-sin, reconstruct their own leadership style, and develop the resilience and insight needed to lead their organizations through future challenges to success.

From Employee to CEO: A Leader's Journey

I joined Utop Group as an entry-level employee and have spent 29 years rising to the role of CEO. Along this journey, I have faced numerous challenges and setbacks, each teaching me valuable lessons about what it takes to lead an organization. In the early days, my goal was simply to fulfill my assigned duties with diligence. However, as time went on, I gradually took on the responsibility of guiding the growth of the organization as a leader. Through this process, I overcame many obstacles and achieved significant personal growth.

Each step of the way, the stories of heroes from *The Three Kingdoms* and Admiral Yi Sun-sin served as a tremendous source of inspiration, offering deep insights into effective leadership.

When I first joined the company, personal achievement was my main focus. Completing my assigned tasks and meeting team goals was my top priority. But as my responsibilities grew, I recognized that my role had evolved beyond simply performing well in my tasks. I now carried the responsibility of uniting the organization and steering it toward a common goal. During my days as an employee, personal accomplishments felt paramount, but today, the organization's success takes precedence. This shift in focus led me to reflect deeply on what it truly means to be a leader.

One of the most essential virtues of a leader is the ability to present a clear vision. Just as Liu Bei pursued the dream of uniting the kingdoms alongside Zhuge Liang, and Admiral Yi Sun-sin defended his country with unwavering commitment, a leader must establish a clear vision and objectives for the organization's direction. However, this vision cannot belong to the leader alone; it must be embraced by everyone in the organization as a shared mission. True leadership is not achieved when a vision remains a personal ambition—it succeeds only when it becomes the organization's collective goal.

1. From Individual Contributor to Leader: The Shift in Focus

The most significant shift I experienced on my leadership journey was moving from focusing on personal accomplishments to prioritizing team success. As an entry-level employee, I was dedicated solely to my responsibilities. But as I grew into a leadership role, I realized that the organization's achievements were far more important than my own. Achieving results remains crucial, but it must be a team effort, with everyone collaborating toward a shared goal.
To achieve this, I found it essential to communicate a clear vision and foster alignment among team members. A leader is not just someone who delegates tasks and sets plans; rather, they must inspire the team and help each member realize their potential. Just as Liu Bei entrusted

Zhuge Liang with significant authority and responsibility, a leader should empower each team member, creating an environment that enables them to thrive. This goes beyond merely seeking results—it involves recognizing each member as an invaluable part of the organization.

2. The Importance of Vision:
Without a Goal, an Organization Loses Direction

Liu Bei faced significant challenges in his quest to unify *The Three Kingdoms*, yet he presented a powerful, long-term vision and dedicated himself wholeheartedly to achieving it. His vision inspired skilled generals like Zhuge Liang, Guan Yu, and Zhang Fei to follow him, not merely because he wielded power, but because he pursued the noble purpose of unifying the kingdoms. Liu Bei was a leader who embodied a greater cause.

Similarly, Admiral Yi Sun-sin had an unyielding mission to protect his country and fought to the end without retreat. His leadership was defined by morality, decisiveness, and an unwavering commitment to his troops. His vision wasn't merely about winning battles—it was about defending his country and its people and securing a future for the next generation. This strong vision and mission inspired absolute loyalty among his soldiers, who were willing to risk their lives to follow him.

For executives as well, a clear vision is essential. Without a defined direction, an organization loses its way and becomes fragmented. Organizations must always move forward with a clear purpose, one that every team member can understand and support. No matter how well-designed a strategy may be, it cannot effectively guide an organization without a vision. Therefore, leaders must continually communicate a long-term goal, ensuring that team members not only understand it but feel a shared commitment toward it.

3. The Leader's Role in Guiding the Organization: From Vision to Strategy

Setting a vision is a leader's first task, but it is not enough. Leaders must also establish concrete strategies and plans to realize that vision.

Just as Liu Bei developed various strategies with Zhuge Liang to achieve the unification of *The Three Kingdoms*, and Admiral Yi overcame unfavorable conditions at the Battle of Myeongnyang by thinking strategically, so too must leaders bring strategic insight to execute their vision. As an executive, I have continually focused on developing strategies centered around the organization's vision, seeking ways to achieve this vision beyond short-term profits and focusing instead on long-term success. A vision without strategy remains unrealized, while strategy without vision loses direction.

The role of a leader is to maintain a balance between

these two elements. It is a leader's mission to support team members in understanding long-term goals through vision and to chart a clear path toward these goals through strategy. Leaders must also ensure that team members not only share in this vision but also adopt it as the organization's overarching objective. Like Liu Bei, who consistently communicated the noble purpose to his team and motivated them to move forward, executives must lead the team in unison, guiding them to pursue a common direction.

4. The Core of Leadership: The Power to Inspire Action

Leadership is the power to move people. A leader must guide team members to reach set goals and support them in realizing their full potential. Just as Zhuge Liang strategized and led Liu Bei's vision, a leader must trust each team member to fulfill their role and provide unwavering support. Leadership goes beyond merely giving directives; it involves motivating and encouraging team members to act willingly toward their goals.

Admiral Yi Sun-sin's troops followed him to the end, not solely due to his military prowess, but because they deeply trusted his moral leadership and sense of responsibility. This trust inspired unwavering loyalty from his soldiers. Leaders must earn the trust of their teams, as only then can members fully commit themselves and perform at their best—a lesson critical for modern executives.

Lessons Executives Should Learn

From the leadership shown by *The Three Kingdoms* rulers and Admiral Yi, we gain insights into the importance of vision, decisiveness, and the power to inspire others. Liu Bei faced many early failures, but he grew by continuously seeking talent and adapting his strategies. The story of his "three visits" to Zhuge Liang highlights the significance of recognizing talent and empowering others to reach their full potential.

Admiral Yi's leadership was rooted in a moral foundation that inspired his troops to risk their lives for him, leading to successive victories on the battlefield. This demonstrates the importance of building trust with employees, as a genuine commitment from executives fosters a unified organization capable of achieving remarkable goals.
Leadership today involves more than issuing instructions. It is the ability to present a compelling vision that team members willingly follow and to instill motivation in them. This book clarifies the essential elements of leadership through concrete examples, illustrating how leaders can inspire those around them.

Decisiveness: The Power to Make Critical Choices

Another indispensable aspect of leadership is decisiveness. Executives face daily decisions that can determine the success or failure of their organization. In *The Three Kingdoms*, Liu Bei accepted responsibility for his critical choices, while Admiral Yi likewise made the right decisions in moments of crisis and bore their consequences.

In modern management, there are frequent moments requiring careful decisions on issues such as market shifts, financial challenges, or internal conflicts. A leader must make swift, accurate decisions and possess the courage to accept responsibility for them. Without decisiveness, an organization risks losing direction and falling into disarray.

As CEO of Utop Group, I have learned that not making a decision can lead to greater failures. There are times when quick decisions are necessary and times when careful deliberation is required. Even if a decision proves wrong, a leader must take responsibility and guide the organization toward a better course.

**Organizational Management:
Placing and Developing People Correctly**

A leader must develop the skill of managing talent effectively. In *The Three Kingdoms*, Liu Bei's selection of Zhuge Liang highlights the importance of recognizing potential and positioning individuals where they can perform to their fullest. Admiral Yi Sun-sin similarly built his forces on a foundation of trust with his subordinates, uniting them and leading the organization to success.

In modern management, people remain the most valuable asset. To lead an organization effectively, leaders must understand each team member's abilities and potential, placing them in roles where they can excel. Providing growth opportunities to help them maximize their potential is equally essential. A leader's role extends beyond mere management; they should act as a coach, supporting the development of their talent.

In my journey, I've always considered how to manage talent effectively and draw out the best from each individual. Proper role allocation and personnel development are crucial factors that determine an organization's success.

Morality and Ethics:
Trust in Leadership Stems from Transparency

In today's business environment, morality and ethics are more crucial than ever. While maximizing profits may have been a company's primary focus in the past, businesses today cannot survive without fulfilling social responsibilities. Organizations that chase only profits risk losing the trust of customers and society, which ultimately threatens long-term growth. Ensuring sustainable success requires transparent and ethical management practices.

The Importance of Moral Leadership:
Lessons from Admiral Yi Sun-sin

Admiral Yi Sun-sin, a hero who saved his country with unyielding morals and convictions, offers a powerful lesson to modern leaders. Even amid war, he upheld strict moral standards, unwavering in his commitment to protect his nation. His sense of responsibility and moral judgment earned the absolute trust of his troops, fueling their dedication to follow him in even the most adverse conditions, like the Battle of Myeongnyang. His soldiers trusted him as a just and fair leader and were willing to risk their lives for him.

Moral leadership remains essential in today's management environment. Leaders must pursue the organization's success while also fulfilling social responsibilities. As shown by Admiral Yi's example, a leader who upholds moral standards earns trust from their team, leading to long-term organizational success. Conversely, leaders who deviate from these principles might achieve short-term success but ultimately risk the organization's collapse by losing trust.
Moral leadership isn't merely a virtue; it's at the heart of effective leadership. Moral leaders operate with honesty and transparency, gaining trust from both internal team members and external stakeholders. Just as Admiral Yi demonstrated, modern leaders must recognize that upholding moral standards and fulfilling social responsibilities are critical for organizational longevity and growth.

Righteous Leadership: Lessons from Liu Bei

Liu Bei is depicted as a righteous and moral leader in *The Three Kingdoms*, with his leadership rooted in personal trust. His sense of justice and fairness allowed him to gain the loyalty of many, attracting talented individuals to pursue his dream of uniting *The Three Kingdoms*. Liu Bei's righteous leadership offers modern executives valuable insights into how to earn and sustain trust.

Today's leaders must also embody righteousness and moral integrity. Trust within an organization is not achieved solely through results; it is cultivated by treating all members with fairness and transparency. Liu Bei earned the loyalty of exceptional talents like Zhuge Liang, Guan Yu, and Zhang Fei because he was a just and fair leader who trusted, valued, and listened to his subordinates.

Executives today likewise need to build trusting relationships with all members, achieved not merely through outcomes or rewards but through an ethical and transparent decision-making process. Only leaders who operate with fairness and uphold moral standards, as Liu Bei did, can earn lasting trust and successfully guide an organization toward long-term success.

Transparency and Ethics: Essential Virtues in Modern Management

Today's companies must do more than pursue profits; they must also fulfill social responsibilities. Transparency and ethical management have become essential virtues in the modern business landscape.
Building trust with customers, employees, and society as a whole is now as vital as generating profits. This is not

just a strategy for enhancing corporate image but a critical factor in enabling sustainable growth.

In the past, many companies focused solely on profit maximization, sometimes overlooking moral standards. However, today's business environment is vastly different. Companies that fail to operate ethically risk losing the trust of customers and markets, which can severely impact their long-term growth.

In a world with heightened transparency and information accessibility through social media, unethical actions by companies are quickly exposed, potentially damaging their reputation in an instant.

Transparency and ethics should be core strategic considerations in management, not merely responses to societal demands. Leaders must consider the impact of their decisions both within and outside the organization, consistently making fair and ethical choices.

Recognizing that building and maintaining trust leads to more significant, sustainable success than relying on unethical shortcuts for short-term gains is crucial.
My management philosophy is also based on transparency and ethical practices. I have always prioritized building trusting relationships with organizational members through honest and transparent decision-making.

Leaders must maintain a responsible attitude toward both

internal and external stakeholders. Ethical management is not only a moral obligation but also a vital strategy for driving the growth of the entire organization.

Trust is Born from Transparency: Ethical Management for Long-Term Success

Executives must deeply consider the impact of their decisions on all members and society and consistently make the right choices. Sacrificing ethical standards for short-term gains ultimately leads to significant losses in the long run. Just as Admiral Yi Sun-sin upheld morality and conviction to save his country, executives who lead with ethical standards will earn genuine trust.

In today's business environment, trust is at the heart of leadership. Transparent management fosters this trust. Customers, employees, and society place their confidence in transparent and ethical leaders, and this trust is integral to a company's sustainable growth and success. The trust built through ethical management is a more valuable asset than short-term achievements. When morality and transparency are central to leadership, companies can achieve stable and sustainable success based on strong societal trust.

Therefore, leaders must make honest, transparent decisions and lead based on trust. Ethical management strengthens an organization, creating a solid foundation for long-term success built on that trust. I have always strived for transparent and ethical management, considering the impact of each decision on all members and society to ensure I make the right choices.

Part 1: The Beginning of Leadership - Vision and Direction

Chapter 1: Fundamentals of Leadership

1.1 What is Leadership? Basic Concepts and Definitions

Leadership may simply be seen as the ability to guide people, yet it encompasses a far more complex and profound meaning. Leadership is the ability to inspire others and provide direction so they can willingly achieve goals. True leadership does not rely on position or authority; instead, a genuine leader earns trust and respect through their vision and actions, empowering others to achieve objectives through their own efforts.

The foundation of leadership rests on three core elements:

Vision:
Leaders must clearly define the direction for their team or organization. Vision includes long-term goals, and the leader establishes specific strategies to bring this vision to life.

Influence:
Leadership is not about coercion but about motivating people through influence. Leaders inspire team members to

commit to goals willingly. Trust and effective communication are essential to this influence.

Responsibility:
Leaders must take accountability for their decisions, accepting both successes and failures, and cultivating a sense of responsibility among team members.

1.2 Leadership Styles: Different Types of Leadership

There are various leadership styles, and a leader's approach often depends on organizational culture, member characteristics, and the context at hand. Understanding different leadership styles enables leaders to apply the most effective approach in each situation.

Charismatic Leadership:
This style relies on charisma and personal appeal to motivate team members. Charismatic leaders often possess a strong vision, guiding and inspiring others through it. For example, Steve Jobs used his charismatic leadership to grow Apple into a global powerhouse.

Transformational Leadership:
Transformational leaders drive organizational change and help members grow. They motivate and support team members to achieve superior outcomes. Nelson Mandela exemplified transformational leadership, inspiring a nation toward change.

Situational Leadership:
This approach involves adapting leadership style to fit different situations. A situational leader adjusts their style based on organizational needs and member capabilities. For example, in a crisis, directive leadership may be necessary, while collaborative leadership may be more suitable for long-term projects.

Servant Leadership:
A servant leader prioritizes supporting team members, fostering an environment that enables their success. This style sees the leader as a supporter who helps each member grow and thrive.

1.3 Core Elements of Leadership: Listening, Communication, and Decisiveness

To be an effective leader, it is not enough to simply set goals. Leaders must convey their vision, listen to team members, communicate effectively, and act decisively.

Listening:
Leaders must be able to listen to their team's perspectives. Zhuge Liang, as Liu Bei's strategist, achieved many victories due to his wisdom and consistent attentiveness to those around him, enabling a clear understanding of situations. Similarly, modern leaders should make decisions based on team insights.

Communication:
Communication is a vital component of leadership. Leaders must articulate their vision and strategy clearly, building trust through effective communication within and outside the organization. Former Intel CEO Andy Grove fostered an environment where everyone could freely express their opinions, allowing for swift and efficient decision-making. His transparent communication helped maintain Intel's competitiveness in the rapidly changing tech industry.

Decisiveness:
Leaders must sometimes make difficult decisions, especially in challenging times. Decisiveness is a crucial quality, as courage is needed to guide an organization through crises. Admiral Yi Sun-sin exemplified decisive leadership by making firm decisions to save his nation amidst crises. Likewise, executives need the capacity to assess risks and bear responsibility for their choices, demonstrating the decisiveness essential to effective leadership.

Chapter 2: Vision and Goal Setting

2.1 The Importance of Vision: Leadership Lessons from Liu Bei and Admiral Yi Sun-sin

What is a Vision?

When asked, "What is a vision?" many might respond with "a goal." Although closely related, vision goes beyond a single goal to define an organization's overarching direction and purpose.

A vision is the leader's dream and the driving force that guides the organization. It determines the organization's trajectory and provides team members with an understanding of why they should move in that direction.

While a goal might relate to a specific project or timeframe, a vision provides a broader perspective—a blueprint for the future that the leader and organization can collectively aim toward. Vision enables leaders to look beyond short-term results and set a clear course for the long-term growth of the organization.

The leadership of Liu Bei and Admiral Yi Sun-sin exemplifies the importance of vision. Both leaders set clear, meaningful aspirations and guided their organizations toward realizing them.

Liu Bei's Vision: Leadership in Pursuit of a Peaceful World

In *The Three Kingdoms*, Liu Bei held a grand vision: to unify the divided kingdoms and create a world of peace. Amidst turbulent times, he constantly pursued this dream of a unified, harmonious world.

Liu Bei's vision wasn't merely about expanding territory or acquiring power; it was deeply rooted in compassion and justice. His purpose-driven vision to build a peaceful world based on humanitarian values became the core of his leadership.

Despite the challenging circumstances he faced, Liu Bei showed incredible resilience and never abandoned his vision, even in the face of countless setbacks and defeats. His vision wasn't only his personal goal; it was a shared aspiration that offered hope and motivation to his followers. Through this vision, he attracted exceptional talents and allies who helped him pave the way toward unification.

Notably, figures like Zhuge Liang, Guan Yu, and Zhang Fei followed Liu Bei not simply because of his power but because they believed in his vision of a peaceful world. This vision, which went beyond short-term power acquisition, demonstrated Liu Bei's commitment to a sustainable world of justice. His unwavering dedication to this cause allowed him to gain the loyalty and trust of his followers, even in the most trying times.

Liu Bei's example offers a crucial lesson for modern leaders: a leader's vision should not be limited to profit generation. It should reflect values and goals that resonate with the organization as a whole, allowing members to feel aligned and motivated by this vision. Leaders must clearly define their vision, as Liu Bei did, so that it becomes a guiding principle for the organization. Team members should understand its value and direction, and work together to bring it to life.

Admiral Yi Sun-sin's Vision: Leadership for Nation and People

Admiral Yi Sun-sin was a moral leader with a well-defined vision. His vision extended beyond battlefield victories to encompass national preservation and the protection of his people.

For Admiral Yi, combat was not just about winning or losing; his vision was to safeguard his homeland and ensure a better future for future generations. This vision of protecting the nation drove him to fight relentlessly, seeing defense of his country as his mission.

His vision and conviction provided him with an unshakeable will, enabling him to stand firm in the face of overwhelming opposition. For example, in the Battle of Myeongnyang, despite being at a disadvantage, Admiral

Yi persisted, driven by his commitment to protect his country. His belief in his cause allowed him to continue fighting without yielding to unfavorable conditions.

Admiral Yi's followers also resonated with his vision for national survival, motivating them to risk their lives in loyalty to him. His leadership and vision serve as valuable lessons for today's executives. Leaders must set goals that encompass the organization's future as well as social value, positioning these goals as shared visions for the organization.

Like Admiral Yi, leaders today should establish long-term visions that consider sustainable growth not only for their organization but also for the broader society to which they belong. And it is essential that this vision resonates with members and stakeholders alike.

A Leader Without Vision Is Like a Ship Lost at Sea

A leader without a vision is like a ship adrift at sea. Vision serves as a compass, clearly pointing the way forward for the organization. A ship without a course will wander aimlessly, eventually sinking, just as an organization without vision falls into confusion, loses direction, and faces inevitable failure.

A leader's vision provides the organization with a sense of purpose, helping members understand why the goal is worth pursuing. Vision is more than just goal-setting; it answers the fundamental question of why the organization exists. It clarifies the organization's purpose and future, allowing members to understand their roles and align with the leader's vision. Without vision, an organization risks losing motivation, leaving members uncertain of the meaning behind their roles. Eventually, even stakeholders may lose trust in such an organization.

Elon Musk's Vision: Leading Global Innovation

A modern example of vision-driven leadership is Elon Musk of Tesla. Musk's vision goes beyond selling electric vehicles; he has put forth an ambitious vision of a sustainable energy society.
This vision surpasses profit motives, aiming to protect the environment and chart a direction for humanity's future. Musk's vision has been the driving force behind Tesla's global innovation. It has not only inspired Tesla's employees and stakeholders but also resonated with customers worldwide, transforming Tesla into a leading technology company rather than just an automaker.

Musk's vision teaches modern leaders an essential lesson: leadership without vision cannot guarantee long-term success. Leaders must always create a clear vision for the future and ensure it resonates with the entire organization, as well as with stakeholders. When a vision extends beyond profit to include social value, an organization can achieve sustainable long-term growth.

The Critical Role of Vision in Modern Management

In today's business environment, vision is indispensable. Leaders who focus solely on short-term goals risk falling behind in a rapidly evolving market. Visionless leadership weakens an organization, ultimately limiting its potential for growth. In contrast, leaders with a clear vision can guide an organization toward lasting success, even amidst change. Vision should be a shared objective that unites the organization as a whole, not merely the leader's personal ambition.

Executives must, like Liu Bei and Admiral Yi Sun-sin, set a clear vision, share it with their team, and work together to build a better future. Only leaders who understand the importance of vision can guide their organization toward long-term success.

2.2 The Process of Setting a Vision: Key Factors for Leaders to Consider

When setting a vision, executives must go beyond wishful goals and provide a clear, achievable direction. Vision is crucial to defining an organization's purpose and trajectory, and leaders should consider several key factors during this process, particularly clarity, inspirational power, and a long-term perspective.

1. Clarity: The Importance of a Concrete Vision

A vision must be clear. Vague and ambiguous visions fail to provide members with a sense of direction, risking organizational confusion. For instance, a vision like "growing the company" is too broad; without specifics on how and in which direction the organization should grow, members may struggle to understand the actual objectives.

A leader should present a clear vision that shows where the organization should be headed and provides specific guidance, motivating team members and helping them understand their roles in achieving it.

Apple's vision, for instance, is "to create the best products in the world that inspire customers." This vision goes beyond simply creating products; it emphasizes delivering a profound impact on customers. Apple's team members focus on how each product can move customers, contributing to Apple's ongoing innovation.

When setting specific goals, leaders should use a clear vision to help members understand their purpose. Ambiguous visions can leave members unsure of their direction, ultimately undermining organizational performance. A clear vision defines the organization's ultimate goals and helps members understand their roles in achieving them.

2. An Inspiring Vision: The Power to Motivate Members

A vision should not only set goals but also inspire and motivate members. It must clearly explain why the goal is important and what values it represents. A vision based solely on numbers or profit may fail to inspire. Instead, a value-driven, inspiring vision enables members to willingly pursue goals with dedication.

For instance, Google's vision, "to organize the world's information and make it universally accessible," goes beyond business or technological goals. This vision represents a meaningful objective to improve global information access, inspiring not only Google employees but also people worldwide.

Google's employees work with the pride of contributing to a project that changes lives, not just working for a company.

An inspiring vision allows members to work toward something greater, fostering empathy for the leader's goals. Leaders should ensure their vision inspires members and motivates them to pursue objectives willingly.

When Liu Bei pursued his vision of uniting *The Three Kingdoms*, his followers were driven not by a quest for power but by the noble cause of building a just and peaceful world. A vision should go beyond simple goal-setting; it should provide members with the motivation to work wholeheartedly toward it.

3. A Long-Term Perspective: Establishing a Realistic and Sustainable Vision

A vision should not focus on short-term objectives but guide the organization's long-term direction. A vision centered only on short-term gains and profits risks failing to ensure organizational sustainability.

Leaders should think deeply about the organization's trajectory with a long-term perspective. A vision must be achicvablc ovcr time and include a clear roadmap for its realization.

For example, Liu Bei set the long-term vision of uniting *The Three Kingdoms*, understanding that it would take time and couldn't be achieved overnight. Liu Bei continually strove toward his goal, recruiting talent and overcoming obstacles. Despite facing many challenges, he never abandoned his vision, showing resilience and perseverance.

Admiral Yi Sun-sin also had a long-term vision to protect his nation, beyond merely winning battles. His dedication to "national survival" enabled him to fight unwaveringly, even under challenging circumstances. This long-term vision inspired his subordinates to follow him loyally, understanding that he fought not for personal gain but for future generations.

When setting a vision, executives must balance short-term goals and a long-term vision. Short-term achievements are important but do not guarantee sustainability. Leaders must consider where the organization should be heading in the long run, outlining a roadmap to realize the vision.

A long-term vision motivates members to pursue goals over time, and it's crucial to help them understand that this vision is realistically achievable.

For instance, Microsoft founder Bill Gates had the vision to popularize personal computers (PCs) in households. At the time, PCs were rarely used in homes, but Gates anticipated technological advances and market changes, predicting PCs would become essential to daily life. Ultimately, his vision led to Microsoft's success and the growth of the PC industry.

Executives setting a long-term vision should realistically analyze the goal's feasibility and devise strategies and plans to increase its attainability. Leaders should also consider whether the vision supports organizational growth and social value, encouraging members to commit to its long-term realization.

A long-term vision should be based on leaders' foresight and realistic judgment, containing a step-by-step roadmap. When these elements are in place, the organization can progress steadily toward the vision, fostering sustained momentum.

2.3 Strategy for Realizing Vision: The Importance of Execution

Setting a vision is an extremely important task for a leader. However, no matter how excellent a vision may be, it is meaningless if it cannot be realized.

The key to realizing a vision lies in strategy and execution. Just as Liu Bei in *The Three Kingdoms* appointed Zhuge Liang to devise a strategy for unifying *The Three Kingdoms*, and Admiral Yi Sun-sin protected the nation by using clear tactics even in adverse combat conditions, managers must also devise an actionable strategy to realize their vision.

The first step to realizing a vision is sharing it with the team. A vision is not just the goal of the leader. Only when the entire organization shares and empathizes with the vision can it be realized in reality. When members understand and resonate with the vision, they become willing to devote themselves to achieving the goal.

Liu Bei and Zhuge Liang: Realizing Vision Through Strategy

In *The Three Kingdoms*, Liu Bei put forth the grand vision of unifying the kingdoms. However, he was only able to work toward this vision by moving beyond ideals and establishing an actionable strategy. Liu Bei appointed the highly capable Zhuge Liang, who crafted precise strategies that enabled them to confront powerful enemies like Cao Cao, who sought control over the Chinese mainland. Liu Bei's vision was not his alone; it became closer to reality through the collaboration and strategic thinking of allies like Zhuge Liang, Guan Yu, and Zhang Fei.

In particular, Zhuge Liang excelled at devising specific tactics and strategies to realize their vision.

For instance, in the Battle of Red Cliffs, Zhuge Liang anticipated the direction of the wind, utilizing a fire attack that allowed them to overcome Cao Cao's overwhelmingly large army.

Together, Liu Bei and Zhuge Liang established phased goals and crafted specific strategies to achieve them. In this way, the strategies they employed were not simply meant to win individual battles but were part of a broader, long-term plan to achieve their grand vision.

This kind of strategic thinking is equally essential in modern management. Leaders need to develop actionable plans that support not only short-term goals but also long-term vision. As demonstrated by Liu Bei and Zhuge Liang, setting phased goals, allocating necessary resources, and clarifying responsibilities are all critical to enabling an organization to progress steadily toward realizing its vision.

Admiral Yi Sun-sin's Tactics: Realizing Vision with Clear Strategy and Execution

The leadership of Admiral Yi Sun-sin illustrates the importance of a clear strategy and the power of execution. Although he held a powerful vision to "defend the nation," vision alone was not enough to win a war. To realize his vision, Admiral Yi crafted meticulous strategies and dedicated himself to executing them precisely.

The Battle of Myeongnyang is a representative example. At that time, Admiral Yi faced the daunting challenge of defending against a Japanese fleet of 330 ships with only 12 of his own. Rather than relying solely on courage or determination, he secured victory through a comprehensive strategy and an unwavering execution plan.

He skillfully utilized the geography, employing tactics to isolate and defeat the enemy ships one by one, ultimately overcoming the overwhelming numbers. Admiral Yi demonstrated that a clear strategy is essential to turning vision into reality.

Additionally, Admiral Yi continually evaluated his tactics even after battles, sharing his vision with his soldiers to boost their morale. He was not a leader who merely issued orders; by actively participating in the battles alongside his subordinates, he earned their trust. It was this executional strength that enabled Admiral Yi to bring his vision of defending the nation to fruition.

The First Stage of Realizing Vision: Sharing the Vision with the Organization

The first stage in realizing a vision is sharing it with the members of the organization. Both Liu Bei and Admiral Yi Sun-sin understood the importance of sharing their vision. Liu Bei clearly communicated the noble cause of "unifying *The Three Kingdoms*" to his subordinates, and Admiral Yi continually communicated his vision of protecting the nation to his soldiers. Rather than holding the goal alone, they ensured that those pursuing it with them understood and shared the vision.

The same applies to modern leaders. A vision is not just for the leader alone. When the entire organization resonates with and internalizes the vision, the chances of realization increase. When members understand the significance of the vision and why it matters, they become motivated to devote themselves to achieving the goal.

For example, Starbucks founder Howard Schultz set the vision of making Starbucks a "third place" rather than just a coffee shop. He shared this vision with his employees, realizing it through specific strategies in store design, employee training, and customer experience. In this way, sharing the vision across the organization and presenting clear strategies to achieve it are vital roles for leaders.

Formulating Concrete Strategies:
The Need for Step-by-Step Execution Plans

To realize a vision, concrete execution plans are essential. As demonstrated by Liu Bei, Zhuge Liang, and Admiral Yi Sun-sin, phased goal setting and strategic resource allocation are indispensable. No matter how grand or inspiring a vision may be, it cannot be realized without specific execution strategies.

Liu Bei, for instance, had the long-term vision of unifying *The Three Kingdoms*. To achieve this vision, he first established control over the Shu region, then proceeded to form alliances and secure victory in the Battle of Red Cliffs. He strategically appointed talented individuals, engaged in diplomatic negotiations, and implemented specific execution plans to advance his vision, countering threats from Cao Cao and Sun Quan.

Admiral Yi Sun-sin also set phased goals in his strategies for protecting the nation. He devised specific tactics to achieve each objective, progressing toward an overall victory while maintaining troop morale and efficiently utilizing resources for maximum impact.

Similarly, modern leaders need actionable and concrete strategies to realize their vision. Key elements for achieving this include the following:

Essential Elements for Modern Leaders

Modern leaders also need to establish specific, actionable strategies to realize their vision. The following elements are indispensable for this:

Setting Phased Goals:
A vision is a large overall picture, but to realize it, it is important to divide it into short-term, medium-term, and long-term goals. By defining specific achievements to be accomplished at each stage, members can track the progress of vision realization and maintain continuous motivation.

Efficient Resource Allocation:
To realize a vision, it is essential to allocate necessary resources such as financial resources, human resources, and technological resources efficiently. Just as Liu Bei meticulously planned the allocation of resources in a strategic way with Zhuge Liang, leaders must create an execution plan that maximizes efficient use of internal and external resources within the organization.

Division of Responsibility and Roles:
Another reason Liu Bei, Zhuge Liang, and Admiral Yi Sun-sin were able to realize their vision was that each person's role and responsibility were clearly divided. Zhuge Liang formulated the strategies, and Liu Bei exercised political leadership. In this way, it is important for members to clearly recognize their roles and fulfill their

corresponding responsibilities.

Execution Power: Translating Strategy into Action:
Finally, execution power is essential. No matter how excellent a strategy may be, it becomes meaningless if it is not executed. Liu Bei and Admiral Yi Sun-sin both demonstrated strong execution power to realize their respective visions. Just as Liu Bei and Zhuge Liang successfully executed their strategy in the Battle of Red Cliffs, Admiral Yi also won victory at the Battle of Myeongnyang with thorough tactics even under disadvantageous conditions. The key to realizing a vision lies in the power to put strategy into action.

A leader must not only formulate strategies but also lead the organization through the process of putting those strategies into action. Just as Admiral Yi himself participated in the battle and commanded the defense of the nation alongside his soldiers, modern leaders should also be leaders who act together with their organization's members.

2.4. Effective Transmission of Vision: Communication Techniques

Setting a vision is the first step in management, but it is not enough on its own. Vision is only realized when the leader clearly communicates it to the organization, and the members empathize with and internalize that vision.

A vision should not end as mere words or goal-setting.

Members need to be motivated to voluntarily participate in realizing the vision, and communication techniques play a crucial role in this process.

A leader must be able to communicate their vision concisely and clearly, ensuring that members understand the purpose and necessity of the vision. It is not enough to simply explain the vision; communication techniques are needed to encourage members to internalize and act upon the vision.

Liu Bei's Case: Transmitting Vision through Belief

Liu Bei, a leader in *The Romance of The Three Kingdoms*, demonstrated exceptional communication skills in conveying his vision. He was always adept at moving people, and the reason was that he presented a clear vision and conveyed it to others with conviction. Liu Bei's vision of uniting *The Three Kingdoms* was not merely a political goal; it was rooted in the belief in building a society based on stability and justice for the people.

To effectively communicate his vision, Liu Bei explained his grand vision of an ideal society to talented individuals like Zhuge Liang and made clear how they could help achieve that goal.

Just as Zhuge Liang was inspired by Liu Bei's vision and formulated strategies for unifying *The Three Kingdoms*, modern leaders must clearly communicate the importance of the vision to their members and show each member how they can contribute to its realization.

A leader needs to explain the reasons and purpose of the vision, creating an environment where members can internalize the goal and take action voluntarily. Through this approach, Liu Bei was able to gain the dedication of talented individuals like Zhuge Liang, Guan Yu, and Zhang Fei. Their voluntary commitment played a decisive role in making Liu Bei's vision a reality.

Admiral Yi Sun-sin: Transmitting Vision Beyond Warfare

Admiral Yi Sun-sin demonstrated extraordinary leadership in communicating a strong belief and sense of mission to his soldiers and the people.
His goal was not simply victory in battle but rather to protect the nation and safeguard the people. Admiral Yi emphasized to his subordinates that this war was not just a battle but a mission to protect the country, instilling empathy and motivation in the hearts of his soldiers.

Modern leaders, like Admiral Yi Sun-sin, need to go beyond focusing on performance and profit. They must clearly communicate why the organization's vision is important. When members accept the vision as more than just a goal—viewing it as a larger social or organizational mission—they strive with greater passion to achieve it.

Steve Jobs: Transmitting Vision Beyond Technology

Steve Jobs was a master communicator when it came to conveying his vision. When introducing new products, he did not simply explain technical features or performance but talked about how the product would change people's lives. He went beyond the technological advantages of the product, describing the future that technology would bring, inspiring employees and customers alike to feel the vision.

Steve Jobs' way of transmitting his vision was not just a product explanation; he presented a grand vision that would transform people's lives.

Similarly, leaders need to present a vision big enough for members to understand the purpose of the vision. Additionally, they must clearly explain how members can contribute to realizing that vision. By conveying the vision clearly and concisely, members can confidently and enthusiastically work towards achieving the goals.

Internalizing Vision through Communication: Encouraging Member Participation

The most crucial factor when leaders communicate a vision is ensuring that members can internalize that vision. The vision should not just exist in the leader's mind; it needs to be conveyed in a way that the entire organization can share and empathize with. Therefore, leaders must go beyond simply explaining the vision and concretely explain how members can contribute to realizing it.

For instance, Liu Bei emphasized to his subordinates the significance of unifying *The Three Kingdoms* and how this would impact the lives of the people, explaining how each of them could contribute to this goal. This approach allowed members to feel a sense of pride and meaning in fighting for a greater goal beyond mere military action, strengthening cohesion and determination in battle.

The Relationship Between Vision and Communication

In the end, simply setting a vision does not guarantee that the organization will move in that direction. Vision realization becomes possible only when effective communication allows members to internalize the vision as their own goal and voluntarily strive to realize it. Leaders like Liu Bei, Admiral Yi Sun-sin, and Steve Jobs all clearly explained the purpose and reasons for their vision, eliciting the voluntary dedication of their members.

Modern leaders should also clearly convey the purpose of the vision based on these communication skills. By fostering an environment where members can actively participate in the process of realizing the vision, leaders can guide their organizations toward success.

Chapter 3: Accurate Decision-Making

3.1 Zhuge Liang's Strategic Thinking: The Judgement of a Leader

In leadership, accurate decision-making is as important as setting a vision. Leaders are responsible for making critical decisions in many situations, and the outcomes of those decisions determine the success or failure of the organization.

The strategic thinking and judgement that Zhuge Liang (Zhuge Liang) displayed alongside Liu Bei (Liu Bei) in *The Romance of The Three Kingdoms* illustrate just how crucial judgement is in leadership. Modern business leaders, too, need to make calm, well-considered decisions amid complex market conditions and ever-changing environments, with such decisions often determining an organization's survival and growth.

A prime example of Zhuge Liang's strategic judgement in *The Romance of The Three Kingdoms* is the Battle of Red Cliffs. This battle was pivotal in *The Romance of the Three Kingdoms*, where the allied forces of Liu Bei and Sun Quan (Sun Quan) defeated Cao Cao's (Cao Cao) vastly larger army. Despite their smaller forces, Liu Bei and Sun Quan were facing a crushing defeat against Cao Cao's massive army. However, Zhuge Liang accurately analyzed the situation and showed outstanding judgement in times of crisis, formulating a brilliant strategy that led to their victory.

The core strategy that enabled him to overcome an unfavorable situation was a fire attack using the wind. Early in the battle, Zhuge Liang carefully analyzed the direction of the wind, using a moment when an unexpected strong wind arose to burn down the enemy fleet. This strategy was a result of meticulous analysis, situational awareness, and accurate decision-making in a crisis. Consequently, Liu Bei and Sun Quan's allied forces managed to triumph over overwhelming odds.

Zhuge Liang's Judgement: Situational Analysis and Calm Decision-Making

The judgement that Zhuge Liang showed in the Battle of Red Cliffs went beyond mere tactical decision-making; it embodied the essence of strategic thinking. He precisely identified the enemy's weaknesses and used a comprehensive analysis of the situation to maximize favorable elements. Specifically, his decisive use of wind—an element of nature—to turn the tide of battle offers valuable lessons for modern business leaders.

Business leaders today face rapidly changing market conditions. The actions of competitors, shifts in consumer trends, and economic instability create situations that resemble a battlefield.

In such times, a leader must quickly and accurately make calm, analysis-based decisions. However, decisions should not rely solely on data analysis. As Zhuge Liang demonstrated, effective decision-making requires a blend of experience and intuition.

Modern business leaders can use advanced tools like big data analytics to forecast market trends and make strategic decisions. But data alone cannot explain everything. Data helps analyze current conditions and spot potential opportunities, but the final decision rests on the leader's insight and judgement.

Just as Zhuge Liang sensed natural changes and strategically utilized them, today's business leaders must seize unseen opportunities in a changing market and make strategic decisions accordingly.

Judgement in Modern Management: Fusion of Data and Intuition

In today's business environment, the judgement of leaders is becoming increasingly important. While advanced technologies like big data and artificial intelligence are used as tools for analysis and forecasting, the final decision-making still lies with the leader. Zhuge Liang's combination of situational analysis and intuition exemplifies the core abilities required of leaders in making decisions today.

Leaders should value intuitive judgement as much as rigorous data analysis. By linking lessons learned from past experience with current data, leaders need to make realistic and practical decisions. As Zhuge Liang demonstrated in the Battle of Red Cliffs, leaders must go beyond numbers to consider the market flow, competitor movements, and shifts in consumer behavior to make sound, comprehensive decisions.

The judgement of a leader is not limited to interpreting data but combines comprehensive situational analysis, future forecasting, and bold decision-making. Zhuge Liang not only predicted the wind's change in the Battle of Red Cliffs but also identified the movements of enemy forces, showing patience to wait for the optimal moment, along with bold decision-making.

Likewise, after thoroughly analyzing market shifts and competitor strategies, business leaders need the courage to make bold decisions at the optimal timing.

Judgement of a Leader: Decision-Making in Crisis

Another of Zhuge Liang's strengths was his decisiveness in crises. He was a leader capable of making bold decisions in the crisis of the Battle of Red Cliffs. This reflects the ability of leaders to make prompt decisions without being paralyzed by fear in difficult situations.

In a crisis, a leader's judgement becomes even more essential. An erroneous decision can lead to losses for the organization, but a well-timed, correct decision can turn a crisis into an opportunity.

Admiral Yi Sun-sin is also renowned for his crisis decision-making. At the Battle of Myeongnyang, facing an enemy force far larger than his own, he accurately assessed the geographical advantage and the weaknesses of his opponents, turning a crisis into victory. Admiral Yi's example shows that crisis situations require not only tactical acumen but also the ability to make calm decisions.

Today's business leaders, like Admiral Yi and Zhuge Liang, need to make the right decisions in times of crisis. Changes in the market, competitive pressures, and unexpected environmental changes can happen at any time. Leaders must make quick, accurate judgements to stabilize the organization and lead it toward growth. Bold decision-making, combined with thorough analysis, is the key to guiding an organization to victory even in a crisis.

Judgement as the Core of Strategic Thinking

Ultimately, the judgement of a leader is at the core of strategic thinking. Just as Zhuge Liang achieved victory in the Battle of Red Cliffs through accurate judgement and strategic thinking, business leaders must also make swift, accurate decisions in complex situations.

The fusion of data analysis and intuitive insight is indispensable in modern management. Moreover, the ability to make decisions in crisis is one of the essential qualities for leaders to guide their organizations toward growth.

3.2. Admiral Yi Sun-sin's Decision-Making: Accurate Judgement in Times of Crisis

The Battle of Hansan Island, led by Admiral Yi Sun-sin, serves as a prime example of the importance of decisiveness in leadership. This battle was a remarkable victory where Admiral Yi defeated the Japanese fleet off the coast of Hansan Island, showcasing the power of the Joseon navy even before the legendary Battle of Myeongnyang.

At the time, Admiral Yi was aware that the Japanese forces were deploying a large fleet to invade Korea and had planned a surprise attack on the Joseon forces near Hansan Island. However, Admiral Yi thoroughly analyzed the enemy's movements, predicted their strategies, and prepared accordingly.

The key decision he made was to use an innovative tactic called the "crane wing formation" to surround the enemy. This strategy involved positioning the fleet in a formation resembling a bird spreading its wings, allowing them to encircle the enemy, block their retreat, and focus their attacks. By employing this tactic, Admiral Yi completely overwhelmed the Japanese forces and secured a decisive victory.

Admiral Yi's decision-making prowess lay in his precise analysis of the enemy's movements, optimal use of the terrain, and his strategic timing in targeting the enemy's weaknesses. When he implemented the crane wing formation, the Japanese forces were trapped, their retreat blocked, and they fell into disarray. Admiral Yi's decision was not merely a matter of courage but was a strategic choice rooted in calm analysis and swift judgement.

The Importance of Decision-Making Leadership in Crisis

In modern management, the ability to make swift and accurate decisions during crises is crucial. Rapidly changing markets, competitive pressures, and unforeseen variables often create situations that demand immediate decision-making from leaders. Without decisiveness, leaders risk escalating a crisis or missing valuable opportunities.

In the Battle of Hansan, Admiral Yi effectively utilized limited resources, identified and countered the strengths of the enemy, and achieved victory. Similarly, managers must be able to make optimal decisions with limited resources. Leaders are often constrained by budgets, talent, and time, and must demonstrate decision-making leadership that can yield the best outcomes within these constraints.

Additionally, delaying decisions in critical situations can lead to even greater losses. Decision-making in management goes beyond simply avoiding risks; at times, it involves taking risks to respond quickly. As Admiral Yi demonstrated in the Battle of Hansan, swift decisions are key to creating opportunities in a crisis. Leaders must make bold, rapid decisions that can determine the survival and growth of their organization, even amid uncertainty.

The Integration of Decisiveness and Strategic Thinking

Decisiveness is not simply about courage; it is the ability to combine thorough analysis with swift execution in leadership. Admiral Yi's victory at the Battle of Hansan exemplifies how careful analysis and bold decisions can defeat an enemy. Business leaders must also apply this kind of leadership, analyzing market shifts and competitor actions in detail and making prompt decisions.

Ultimately, decision-making in crisis situations is a critical factor in a leader's success or failure. Just as Admiral Yi overwhelmed the enemy with the crane wing formation, modern business leaders must make realistic and logical decisions in challenging situations to achieve optimal results.

Satya Nadella: Decisive and Innovative Leadership

Admiral Yi Sun-sin's decision-making and leadership continue to offer valuable lessons for modern leaders. Satya Nadella, CEO of Microsoft, is a prime example of a leader who used decisive action to transform the company's direction, turning a crisis into an opportunity. Upon becoming CEO in 2014, Nadella made the bold decision to shift the company from its traditional software sales structure to a cloud-focused strategy.

At the time, Microsoft was heavily dependent on sales of its Windows operating system and Office programs, but the growing limitations of the traditional model and the rapid rise of cloud technology were becoming clear. Nadella calmly analyzed this situation and made a critical decision to shift to a cloud-centered business model. This decision entailed risks, as it fundamentally altered Microsoft's long-standing business model, but it ultimately enabled Microsoft to become a global leader in cloud services.

Nadella's decisiveness was not only the result of analyzing market trends but also of predicting future developments and acting quickly. This mirrors how Admiral Yi analyzed the enemy's weaknesses, acted swiftly, and overcame the crisis with his strategy.
Modern business leaders must display a similar level of decisiveness. Anticipating market shifts and making strategic decisions that stay one step ahead of competitors are essential factors for an organization's success.

Elements of Decisiveness:
Analysis, Strategy, and Execution

Decisiveness is not simply about making decisions quickly. It requires thorough analysis and an understanding of the situation, followed by effective execution. Admiral

Yi's decisive actions at the Battle of Hansan were based on meticulous analysis of both his own and the enemy's movements, and his strategic judgement in using the terrain to his advantage. Similarly, Zhuge Liang, in the Battle of Red Cliffs, used situational analysis and decisiveness to implement a fire attack strategy utilizing the wind. Business leaders, when making strategic decisions, should combine comprehensive situational analysis with a clear execution plan.

Decisiveness includes the courage and ability to predict outcomes and take responsibility for those outcomes. Leaders must be prepared to make the best choice even in uncertain situations and be accountable for the impact of their choices on the organization. Bold decisions may sometimes involve risks, but they can be the key to seizing opportunities in crises. Modern business leaders must be prepared to make strategic decisions that combine analysis and intuition without fear of risk.

The Harmony of Vision and Judgement

Decisiveness is at the core of leadership and is an essential tool for realizing the vision that guides an organization toward success. Vision provides clarity on where leaders should direct their organizations, while judgement and decisiveness are essential for bringing that vision to life. Through their leadership, Liu Bei and Admiral Yi Sun-sin both employed clear vision and swift, accurate judgement to lead their organizations to success, even in

the face of crises.
Modern leaders are no different. While setting a vision and devising a strategy for achieving it are critical, so are the judgement and decisiveness needed to make correct decisions throughout the process. Without vision, an organization risks losing direction, and without judgement and decisiveness, the vision remains unfulfilled.

Just as Admiral Yi used calm judgement and swift decision-making to overcome overwhelming odds in a crisis, business leaders, too, can guide their organizations to success by making bold decisions in challenging situations.

Part 2: Organizational Management – The Power of Talent and Communication

Chapter 1: The Importance of Talent

1.1. Why Talent Matters: Learning from the Cases of *The Romance of The Three Kingdoms* and Admiral Yi Sun-sin on the Power of Talent Management

When reading *The Romance of The Three Kingdoms*, one of the most striking aspects is how the course of history is greatly altered by the abilities of each character and by the roles to which they were assigned. Liu Bei understood well that he was neither a powerful general nor a military genius. Therefore, he realized early on that having outstanding talent was essential to realizing his dream of unifying *The Three Kingdoms*. One of the most important aspects of leadership demonstrated by Liu Bei in *The Romance of The Three Kingdoms* was securing the best talent—and that talent was none other than Zhuge Liang.

Zhuge Liang was not just an exceptional strategist; he was the key advisor who transformed Liu Bei's vision into concrete, actionable plans. Without Zhuge Liang, Liu Bei's dreams would have remained as idealistic aspirations. But Zhuge Liang turned that vision into an achievable strategy, helping Liu Bei gradually expand his influence. Zhuge Liang supported Liu Bei not only in military strategy but also in diplomatic and political decisions, filling in the gaps where Liu Bei lacked expertise. This allowed Liu Bei to establish himself as a significant ruler in *The Romance of The Three Kingdoms*.

The Role of Zhuge Liang: The Importance of Proper Delegation of Authority

When Liu Bei appointed Zhuge Liang, one of the most important aspects of his leadership was the delegation of appropriate authority and responsibility. Zhuge Liang received Liu Bei's full trust, which empowered him to fully demonstrate his abilities. Knowing his own military limitations, Liu Bei entrusted Zhuge Liang with full authority, enabling him to carry out independent strategies. This serves as an exemplary case of what modern management would call "placement of the right person in the right role" and "delegation of authority."

In today's business management, the importance of talent lies precisely in this point. Today's business environment no longer allows a single person to solve everything alone. Organizational leaders need to place experts in various fields in the right positions and provide them with the authority to resolve issues independently.

Elon Musk's leadership at Tesla is similar. He has a strong focus on technology development and innovation, yet he does not develop all technologies himself. Instead, Musk finds top engineers capable of realizing his vision and grants them autonomy to create innovative products.

What is important in this process is to trust the talent and create an environment where they can fully utilize their abilities. This is akin to how Liu Bei entrusted Zhuge Liang with full authority. It is a method by which leaders acknowledge their own limits and delegate responsibility and authority to others in order to achieve the best results.

Admiral Yi Sun-sin's Talent Management: Placing the Right People in the Right Roles

Admiral Yi Sun-sin also demonstrated the importance of talent management through his battlefield leadership. He accurately understood the abilities and personalities of each commander and soldier, even during combat, and he displayed excellent leadership by placing them in appropriate positions.

Victory in battle is not solely determined by superior weapons or numbers but largely influenced by people's abilities and roles. Admiral Yi Sun-sin fully understood this principle and demonstrated the ability to place the right people in the right roles accordingly.

For instance, in sea battles, he assigned experienced generals to missions that required quick judgment and decisive action and appointed the most trustworthy individuals to execute major strategies. This demonstrates leadership that not only selects capable individuals but also places them in positions suited to their abilities.

Admiral Yi Sun-sin's arrangement of soldiers and division of roles was a decisive factor in the outcome of battles, revealing his keen insight into evaluating people.

Talent Management in Modern Management

This type of talent management also provides valuable lessons in modern business management. Managers must accurately understand the capabilities of their team members and assign them tasks in which they excel. They must also offer continuous feedback and support to ensure that each individual can faithfully fulfill their role.

Just as Admiral Yi Sun-sin assessed the abilities of his soldiers and assigned roles accordingly, modern leaders are expected to manage in a way that places each member in the position where they can achieve the best results.

The Importance of Talent Management in Modern Business: The Case of Brian Chesky

Brian Chesky, the founder and CEO of Airbnb, is a leader who has demonstrated the importance of talent management in growing his company.

Airbnb pioneered the new concept of the sharing economy, going beyond the traditional hotel industry. In this process, Brian Chesky devoted himself to securing the best talent who could drive innovative growth and creating an environment where they could exercise autonomy.

Airbnb began as a startup and expanded globally, where a flexible organizational structure adapted to rapidly changing environments was crucial. Brian Chesky created a culture that encouraged employees to propose creative ideas and empowered them to implement them, ultimately establishing the company as a global platform.

One prominent aspect of his leadership is his attentiveness to employees' voices, entrusting them with authority and responsibility so that they could independently address issues. As Airbnb expanded into new markets, Chesky encouraged free-thinking among employees, assigning each person clear responsibilities, and leading efficient operations.

Chesky's leadership emphasizes not just delegation of authority but also continuous feedback and support, ensuring that talent achieves the best results. He built a culture where members take pride in their roles and are motivated as they achieve individual goals.

**Brian Chesky's Talent Management:
A Balance of Autonomy and Responsibility**

Brian Chesky emphasized both autonomy and responsibility in Airbnb's growth. He supported employees to make their own decisions while also encouraging them to take responsibility for those decisions. This approach of placing trust in employees is similar to Liu Bei's delegation of full authority to Zhuge Liang.

Chesky has respected various ideas from his employees, ensuring that they align with the company's vision and goals, and adjusting them into feasible forms. By fostering creativity within the organization while instilling a sense of responsibility, he created an environment where employees could actively contribute to the company's growth. This is a core element of talent management in modern business.

Talent Management in the Growth of Airbnb

Brian Chesky's talent management strategy played a vital role in Airbnb's successful expansion into global markets. As the company scaled, Chesky appropriately delegated authority, allowing employees to demonstrate their expertise, respected their creative thinking, and built a culture based on autonomy.

Notably, when Airbnb faced crises, Chesky maximized employee abilities to address issues. For example, during the COVID-19 pandemic, which severely impacted the travel industry, he communicated directly with employees, listened to their ideas, and developed new strategies. As a result, Airbnb was able to adapt swiftly to the crisis and turn it into an opportunity.

The Essence of Talent Management

The power of talent management demonstrated by Liu Bei in *The Romance of The Three Kingdoms*, Admiral Yi Sun-sin, and modern leader Brian Chesky lies at the heart of leadership. The essential role of a leader is to find the best talent, empower them with appropriate authority and autonomy, and create an environment where they can produce results. Talent is a critical factor in determining the success or failure of an organization, and a leader's role is to establish an environment where they can fully realize their potential.

Managers should accurately assess their team's abilities, assign each member to roles in which they excel, and focus on talent management by providing continuous support and feedback to achieve the best results. This is the key to leading an organization to success.

1.2. Learning the Importance of Talent Recruitment from the "Three Visits" Story in *The Romance of The Three Kingdoms*: Application to Modern Management

The story of the "Three Visits" describes how Liu Bei went to visit Zhuge Liang (Kongming) three times to persuade him to join his cause, symbolically emphasizing the importance of talent recruitment. This tale is not just a historical legend; it also provides a valuable lesson on talent acquisition in modern management.

Liu Bei did not simply seek to recruit Zhuge Liang based on his abilities alone. He made an effort to deeply understand Zhuge Liang's character, values, and vision to assess whether he would be a suitable partner in realizing his dream of unifying *The Three Kingdoms*.

In this process, Liu Bei attempted to confirm whether Zhuge Liang's vision and philosophy aligned with his own leadership. This went beyond simply evaluating ability; it was a core process of talent recruitment, highlighting the importance of talent recruitment in modern management.

Lesson from the "Three Visits": Sincere Efforts in Talent Recruitment

The story of the "Three Visits" is more than just a tale of Liu Bei's three attempts to bring Zhuge Liang into his fold. It symbolizes the need for a sincere and genuine approach in talent recruitment.

Liu Bei highly valued Zhuge Liang's wisdom and strategic abilities, but he considered something beyond these qualities as well. He assessed whether Zhuge Liang was trustworthy and whether their visions were compatible. In other words, Liu Bei did not merely hire him based on his abilities alone. Liu Bei put considerable effort into evaluating if Zhuge Liang was the right partner to help realize his dream.

This approach to talent recruitment provides an important lesson for modern management. Exceptional talent is not simply found through job postings; it requires a leader's own sincere attitude and deep insight.

Talent Recruitment in Modern Management: The Case of Reed Hastings at Netflix

Reed Hastings, CEO of Netflix, has taken a very careful approach to recruiting and managing talent to drive the company's growth as a leader in the video streaming industry. He has valued not only the technical skills and backgrounds of candidates but also their cultural fit and innovative mindset when seeking talent who could lead the company's growth.

Netflix emphasizes a creative and autonomous environment, and Hastings has dedicated himself to creating a space where employees can freely propose ideas and experiment. He evaluates talent not only by their abilities but also by how well they fit into Netflix's innovative culture and can harmonize and grow with the team.

Reed Hastings has built a results-oriented culture in which employees are given the autonomy and responsibility to manage and make decisions about their work. This approach is similar to how Liu Bei trusted Zhuge Liang's vision and values, granting him full authority.

Talent Recruitment at Netflix: Valuing More Than Just Technical Skills

Netflix, in hiring employees, evaluates not only technical skills but also how well candidates align with the company's culture and values. Finding individuals who think innovatively and possess autonomy is one of Netflix's keys to success. Reed Hastings has continually sought out creative and independent talent, not only for Netflix's technology side but also to lead the industry in content creation. He has fostered a culture where employees can freely express their opinions and test new ideas. This trust-based management has been a critical factor in Netflix's success in the fiercely competitive media industry.

Netflix's hiring process, much like Liu Bei's repeated efforts to win over Zhuge Liang, is a careful and thorough process that seeks to find top talent and ensure they align with the company's vision.

The Importance of Sincerity in Talent Recruitment: Building Trust Between Managers and Organizations

A manager's sincerity is essential in talent recruitment. Candidates carefully observe the true intentions of the organization looking to hire them.

They discern whether the leader is merely looking for skilled talent for short-term results or whether they genuinely care about the candidate's growth and success with a long-term vision.

Reed Hastings based his approach on Netflix's long-term vision and innovative culture, providing growth opportunities for talent and creating an environment where employees could autonomously achieve results. This sincerity-based approach has been a critical factor in Netflix's success in the global market.

When leaders approach talent recruitment with sincerity and support their growth, trust is built within the organization, which leads to long-term success.

Post-Recruitment Growth:
Providing Opportunities at Netflix

Recruiting talent is only the beginning. Once top talent is found, it is essential to provide opportunities within the organization for them to grow. Netflix offers a free environment where employees can self-manage their careers along with continuous feedback.

Reed Hastings supports employees to continuously learn and develop their careers, allowing Netflix to achieve sustained innovation. This environment helps exceptional talent grow into leaders within Netflix.

Just as Liu Bei persisted with sincere efforts to bring Zhuge Liang on board in the story of the "Three Visits," modern leaders should approach talent recruitment with careful and genuine efforts, providing a growth environment afterward. By successfully following this process, organizations can achieve long-term sustainable results.

1.3. Talent Management:
Proper Placement of Talent in *The Romance of The Three Kingdoms* and Admiral Yi Sun-sin

In *The Romance of The Three Kingdoms*, one of the essential aspects of Liu Bei's leadership was not only recruiting excellent talent but also his ability to place them appropriately. Liu Bei not only acquired an outstanding talent in Zhuge Liang but also positioned him where his abilities could be maximally utilized, achieving effective talent management.

Zhuge Liang became Liu Bei's right hand as a tactical and strategic advisor, with Liu Bei granting him the autonomy to make strategic decisions and placing full trust in him. This distribution of trust and responsibility was a crucial factor in Zhuge Liang's ability to perform at his highest level.

Furthermore, Liu Bei did not restrict Zhuge Liang's role to that of a mere military advisor but also utilized him as a political negotiator. Zhuge Liang played a strategic partner role in shaping not only military tactics but also the state's vision. His decisiveness and strategic judgment were crucial in Liu Bei's expansion efforts. By granting Zhuge Liang sufficient autonomy, Liu Bei created an environment where he could freely exercise his abilities. In this way, Liu Bei was able to overcome numerous crises and establish a significant position within the Chinese continent.

Zhuge Liang: A Success Story in Talent Placement and Granting Autonomy

The case of Zhuge Liang illustrates two important principles in talent management: the importance of proper placement and the granting of responsibility and autonomy.

The first principle is placing the right person in the right position, while the second is providing responsibility and authority. By allowing Zhuge Liang autonomy in making strategic decisions, Liu Bei enabled him to fully exercise his talents.

First Principle: Placing Talent in the Right Position

Liu Bei accurately recognized Zhuge Liang's strategic abilities and positioned him as a strategic advisor. Zhuge Liang was not only an advisor but a central figure in leadership, encompassing military strategy, diplomacy, and political judgment. Liu Bei leveraged Zhuge Liang in the fields where he excelled and supported him to achieve the best results.

Second Principle: Granting Responsibility and Authority

Another critical principle in Zhuge Liang's success story is the granting of responsibility and authority. Liu Bei demonstrated full trust in Zhuge Liang's ability to make significant decisions, empowering him to independently formulate and implement strategies. This went beyond the role of a mere advisor, granting Zhuge Liang autonomy as an essential leader working toward Liu Bei's expansion and the unification of *The Three Kingdoms*.

For example, in major battles like the Battle of Red Cliffs, Zhuge Liang was able to independently formulate and execute battle plans based on his strategic judgment. Liu Bei gave Zhuge Liang the responsibility to make strategic decisions and the authority to lead political negotiations and military operations. This division of responsibility and authority enabled Zhuge Liang to achieve the best results, contributing to Liu Bei's success.

The Importance of Granting Responsibility and Authority in Modern Management

In modern management, the principle of granting responsibility and authority remains essential. Leaders should empower each team member to make decisions and take action autonomously. This allows them to achieve creative and independent results. Leadership that entrusts responsibility and demonstrates trust is a crucial factor in promoting autonomy and motivation in talent management.

Sun Quan's Leadership: Understanding Each Person's Strengths and Assigning the Right Roles

Sun Quan's talent management in *The Romance of The Three Kingdoms* is a prime example of exemplary leadership. Sun Quan assigned the most suitable roles to exceptional talents like Zhou Yu and Lu Su, supporting them so that they could achieve maximum results. Zhou Yu demonstrated exceptional skill in military strategy, and with his help, Sun Quan achieved a great victory against Cao Cao's army in the Battle of Red Cliffs.

Meanwhile, Lu Su was an individual with excellent diplomatic skills, and Sun Quan appointed him to handle political negotiations and strengthen alliances with other states, thereby maximizing his diplomatic talents. Sun Quan accurately understood the strengths and characteristics of each individual, positioning them so they could fully leverage their abilities. This is an exemplary case demonstrating the importance of leadership in talent management.

Sun Quan's talent placement strategy offers significant lessons for modern business leaders. Managers need to accurately understand each member's strengths and weaknesses and assign them tasks where they can best showcase their strengths. Additionally, it's crucial to provide continuous support so that team members can fulfill their roles responsibly.

Admiral Yi Sun-sin's Leadership: Strategy for Placement Based on Soldiers' Abilities

Admiral Yi Sun-sin was an outstanding leader who demonstrated a strategy of placing soldiers based on their abilities and experience in combat. He deeply understood that success in battle does not solely rely on the number of troops or weapons but is significantly influenced by the abilities of the soldiers. Admiral Yi created an environment where his soldiers could fully utilize their roles, considering each individual's strengths and weaknesses, thereby drawing out the best performance from his troops.

In battles, he strategically placed experienced generals in key positions and appointed reliable individuals to carry out essential long-term strategies. This approach went beyond merely selecting talented individuals, as it showcased his ability to accurately identify each soldier's strengths and provide an environment where they could operate with maximum efficiency.

This strategy also offers critical lessons for maximizing member capabilities in modern management. Leaders must accurately understand their team members' abilities and assign them to positions where they can deliver the best results. Moreover, it is essential to provide an environment where team members can continue to grow.

Placing Talent in the Right Roles in Modern Management: The Case of IBM

In modern management, placing talent in the right roles has a significant impact on organizational success. Business leaders must aim to accurately evaluate employees' strengths and weaknesses and place them in positions where they can achieve maximum results. To do so, it's essential to analyze employees' personalities, experiences, and skills comprehensively and provide them with opportunities to grow within the organization.

IBM has introduced an AI-driven human resource management system to analyze employees' achievements, abilities, and career development plans and develop suitable placement strategies. Through this, IBM maximizes organizational efficiency and provides an environment where employees can grow. Data-driven talent management systems have become essential tools in modern management, playing a crucial role in accurately evaluating employee performance and abilities and establishing appropriate placement strategies accordingly.

In this way, placing the right people in the right roles is indispensable for the success of modern organizations. By applying the lessons learned from *The Romance of The Three Kingdoms* and Admiral Yi Sun-sin's examples to modern management, leaders can create environments where employees can maximize their potential, thereby leading the organization to success.

The Importance of Leadership in Assigning Talent to the Right Roles

Leadership in assigning talent to the right roles provides valuable lessons from *The Romance of The Three Kingdoms* and Admiral Yi Sun-sin's example. Leaders like Liu Bei, Sun Quan, and Admiral Yi accurately understood the abilities of their team members and assigned them to positions where they could achieve the greatest results, leading their organizations to success.

Similarly, modern business leaders need to accurately assess the abilities of their team members and assign tasks in which they excel. It is also important to create an environment where they can work autonomously and fulfill their responsibilities. To achieve this, it's essential to provide continuous feedback and support. Leadership in placing talent in the right roles is a critical factor for organizational success, and its implementation contributes to improving the overall performance of the organization.

1.4. Retention of Talent: The Importance of Trust as Demonstrated by Zhuge Liang and Admiral Yi Sun-sin

Retaining talent is a more challenging task than recruiting it. Even if a company discovers and hires exceptional talent, this alone does not guarantee success. Establishing an environment where talent remains within the organization and can produce long-term results is an even more critical task.

The stories of *The Romance of The Three Kingdoms* and Admiral Yi Sun-sin illustrate an essential lesson: trust is key to retaining talent. Liu Bei and Admiral Yi led their organizations to success through deep, trusting relationships with their subordinates. In modern management, this trust also functions as a crucial factor in retaining talent.

The Trust Between Liu Bei and Zhuge Liang: A Case of Successful Talent Retention

Liu Bei established a deep bond of trust with Zhuge Liang and entrusted him completely. Following the "Three Visits" to acquire Zhuge Liang, Liu Bei not only gave him a role as a strategic advisor but assigned him a significant position within the organization, showing absolute faith in his judgments and decisions.

Liu Bei allowed Zhuge Liang to feel that he was not merely an advisor to execute commands but a colleague and partner in pursuing their shared goals. This mutual trust became the foundation for Zhuge Liang's unwavering dedication to realizing Liu Bei's vision to the end.

Zhuge Liang shared Liu Bei's vision and committed all his efforts to realize it. This dedication wasn't simply a matter of following Liu Bei's leadership; it was possible because Zhuge Liang was convinced of Liu Bei's complete trust in him.

Zhuge Liang fully understood the responsibility and authority Liu Bei had entrusted him with, which became a motivating factor in maximizing his capabilities. Trust was the key element enabling Zhuge Liang to maintain his partnership with Liu Bei and remain loyal until the end.

Admiral Yi Sun-sin's Trust in His Subordinates: Loyalty and Success in Battle

Similarly, Admiral Yi Sun-sin achieved success in battle through deep trust in his subordinates. His sense of responsibility and dedication inspired even greater trust from his men. Admiral Yi consistently took responsibility for his role and duties, and he also trusted his subordinates to fulfill theirs. This mutual trust transformed into loyalty among his troops, who were willing to risk their lives for him.

Admiral Yi was not merely a commander who issued orders; he gained his soldiers' loyalty even in unfavorable battle conditions by fostering mutual trust. For instance, in critical battles such as the Battle of Myeongnyang, his subordinates fought with their lives on the line, driven by the trust Admiral Yi placed in them. This illustrates how crucial trust is in talent retention within an organization. His troops felt a profound sense of responsibility in carrying out their roles and devoted themselves to realizing Admiral Yi's vision until the end.

The Importance of Talent Retention in Modern Management

In today's management environment, retaining talent is a vital element determining a company's success. Today's top talent does not remain in a company merely for high salaries or benefits. They desire to feel valued in an organization that offers growth opportunities and recognizes their contributions. Talent retention is essential to an organization's long-term success, and trust forms a crucial foundation for drawing out loyalty and dedication from employees.

When talented individuals are confident that they are recognized as valuable within the organization, they are more likely to stay long-term. When they feel their role is vital to the organization and they are given opportunities for growth, they will put forth even greater efforts to produce high results. Therefore, it is crucial for management to establish trust by providing transparent communication, regular feedback, and fair evaluation.

For example, Netflix offers a workplace environment where employees are free to express their creativity, and it fairly rewards their achievements. Netflix's talent management policies are centered on a trust-based management philosophy, making it a desirable place for exceptional talent to work long-term.

The Role of Executives in Building Trust

Executives need to take various approaches to build a trusting relationship with their talent.

1. Transparent Communication
Transparent communication is the first step in building trust with talent. By openly sharing the decision-making process and organizational goals, executives enable employees to clearly understand how their role contributes to the organization's success. This enhances employees' motivation to fulfill their responsibilities more effectively.

2. Regular Feedback
Regular feedback is extremely important in talent management. Executives should continuously monitor employees' performance and provide constructive feedback to create growth opportunities. By actively listening to employees' challenges and opinions during the feedback process, executives can build stronger trust with them. This helps employees feel valued within the organization, leading to even greater achievements.

3. Fair Evaluation and Compensation
Fair evaluation and compensation are critical elements for building trust. When employees are recognized for their achievements based on fair evaluation standards and receive corresponding compensation, they feel trusted and valued by the organization. Such a fair reward system plays an important role in retaining talent, motivating em-

ployees to willingly contribute to the organization.

Providing Opportunities for Retention and Growth

Another essential element for talent retention is providing growth opportunities. When employees are given chances to improve their skills within the organization, they feel inclined to stay longer. Educational programs, mentoring, and leadership development opportunities help employees advance their careers within the organization and grow as future leaders.

Companies like Facebook operate a variety of educational and leadership development programs for employees' career growth. These growth opportunities serve as vital motivation for employees to stay in the organization long-term and plan their futures within the organization. By continuously providing opportunities for talent to grow within the organization, executives can earn their loyalty.

Trust-Based Talent Retention Strategy

Talent retention is essential for an organization's success, and trust plays an extremely important role in achieving it. As seen in the cases of Liu Bei and Zhuge Liang in *The Romance of The Three Kingdoms* and Admiral Yi Sun-sin, trust is the foundation that enables talent to remain dedicated to the organization until the end.

Modern executives also need to establish a trusting relationship with employees through transparent communication, regular feedback, fair evaluation and compensation, and by providing growth opportunities, helping them stay within the organization for the long term.

Trust-based management not only retains excellent talent within the organization but also serves as a crucial motivation for them to achieve the best results. Talent retention is a cornerstone strategy for a company's long-term success, and executives must build a trust-centered talent management strategy to achieve it.

Chapter 2: Trust and Communication

2.1 The Power of Trust: Learning from Liu Bei and Admiral Yi Sun-sin on the Importance of Building Trust within an Organization

The deep trust Liu Bei and Admiral Yi Sun-sin built with their subordinates played a decisive role in their success. Liu Bei understood well that, as a leader, by placing trust in his subordinates, he could inspire their loyalty and dedication. Liu Bei not only extended this trust to close aides like Zhuge Liang, Guan Yu, and Zhang Fei but also used trust as a basis for every decision made in leading his entire army.

This trust allowed strategists like Zhuge Liang to remain fully devoted to Liu Bei and to maintain loyalty even in times of crisis. Throughout the trust-building process, Liu Bei consistently demonstrated open communication and respect. His ongoing communication with his subordinates, willingness to listen to their opinions, and collaborative decision-making were crucial elements in establishing trust.

For example, Liu Bei kept his decision-making process transparent and consistent, allowing his subordinates to rely on his leadership. This trustworthiness was a factor that encouraged talents like Zhuge Liang, Guan Yu, and Zhang Fei to remain loyal to Liu Bei and respect him as a leader, even in moments of crisis.

Similarly, Admiral Yi Sun-sin gained deep trust from his subordinates through his honesty and transparency. He led by example on the battlefield, inspiring his men with his dedication. Yi Sun-sin consistently took responsibility for his duties and established himself as a leader whom his men could trust and follow. His decisive leadership, particularly during extreme situations like the Battle of Myeongnyang, inspired his subordinates to risk their lives in loyalty.

In modern management, building trust within an organization is also a critical factor. In organizations lacking trust, conflicts and confusion can arise, preventing members from realizing their full potential. Executives must foster trust within the organization through transparent decision-making processes and consistent behavior. This requires leaders to maintain consistency in their words and actions, building a relationship of trust where team members believe in and follow their leader's decisions.

Rather than issuing unilateral orders, executives should listen to team members' opinions, establish communication frameworks that integrate these perspectives, and gradually build trust. Furthermore, transparent information sharing and fair evaluations are foundational to trust. The importance of trust, as demonstrated by Liu Bei and Admiral Yi Sun-sin, is an indispensable element in successful organizational management, even today.

2.2 Communication Skills:
Leadership in Communication as Shown by Zhuge Liang and Admiral Yi Sun-sin

Zhuge Liang was not just a strategist but a leader with excellent communication skills. He communicated smoothly with Liu Bei and his subordinates, guiding them to act based on accurate information. Zhuge Liang regularly communicated with Liu Bei, clearly understanding his vision, and made no hesitation in proposing strategies to realize that vision. Thanks to his strategic communication, Liu Bei's army could operate cohesively, carrying out consistent strategies even during times of crisis.

The communication style between Liu Bei and Zhuge Liang was especially significant. Zhuge Liang did not merely follow Liu Bei's orders passively; instead, he shared Liu Bei's vision and openly discussed the best methods to achieve it. Liu Bei placed full trust in Zhuge Liang, creating an environment where Zhuge Liang could make independent decisions and act accordingly. Liu Bei transparently shared his thoughts and vision, and Zhuge Liang then crafted strategies based on them.

This trust-based communication was a key factor that enabled Liu Bei's army to act consistently and achieve success during various crises depicted in *The Romance of The Three Kingdoms*. Smooth communication allowed Zhuge Liang to quickly grasp Liu Bei's intentions and make the best decisions accordingly.

Admiral Yi Sun-sin also placed great importance on communication with his subordinates. Before battles, he held thorough discussions with his men, formulated tactics, and clearly explained the necessity of each battle. By candidly conveying his thoughts and plans, Admiral Yi Sun-sin inspired his subordinates to trust and follow him.

Yi Sun-sin's communication style was one of the reasons he gained such deep trust from his men. He consistently led from the front, instilling confidence in his subordinates, and through honest and transparent communication, he ensured their unwavering loyalty. Even in extreme situations like the Battle of Myeongnyang, his subordinates responded to the trust and communication Yi Sun-sin had demonstrated, risking their lives to follow him. Yi Sun-sin's ability to explain his tactics and the reasons for battle to his troops significantly contributed to his reputation as a successful leader.

In modern management, effective communication is also essential to successful organizational operations. Through clear and transparent communication, executives must ensure that each member understands the organization's goals and vision, as well as their own roles. Additionally, it is crucial to establish a communication system that listens to members' opinions and incorporates them into the organizational framework.

Executives must not only communicate information but must also ensure that members resonate with the organization's goals and fully understand their roles through consistent communication. Through clear and transparent communication, members can feel motivated, fostering a commitment to contributing to the organization's goals.

The communication leadership demonstrated by Zhuge Liang and Admiral Yi Sun-sin offers valuable lessons to modern executives. They were not merely leaders who issued orders but exhibited exceptional communication abilities that helped achieve organizational goals by fostering smooth communication with their subordinates.

2.3. The Outcomes of Communication: The Synergy of Trust and Communication

Trust and communication form a complementary relationship that enables the highest level of achievement within an organization. Leaders like Liu Bei and Zhuge Liang, and General Yi Sun-sin and his troops, all leveraged the synergy between trust and communication to bring out the best results. They maintained profound mutual trust and engaged in constant communication to contribute to the goals of their respective organizations.

Through open communication with Zhuge Liang, Liu Bei was able to formulate precise strategies, and General Yi Sun-sin led his troops to success through consistent communication. In this way, trust combined with communication allows an organization to operate cohesively and stay resilient, even in the face of crises.

This synergy between trust and communication also has a powerful impact in modern business management. Leaders today must cultivate trust through clear communication with their teams, thus maximizing organizational outcomes. For example, Google has fostered employee trust through open communication and transparent management, leading to groundbreaking results.

Google shares decision-making processes transparently with employees, listens to their opinions, and aligns them with the organization's goals. As a result, employees build trust with the leadership and are empowered to achieve self-driven success. Google's culture, rooted in trust and open communication, has played a major role in establishing the company as one of the most innovative in the world.

Today's leaders must create environments where team members can fully realize their potential through the synergy of trust and communication. When management builds a foundation of trust and clearly communicates with team members, individuals understand their roles, trust leadership decisions, and willingly commit themselves to the organization's goals, ultimately achieving outstanding results.

In conclusion, an organization built on trust and communication empowers members to increase their motivation autonomously, thereby driving the organization's long-term success.

Part 3: Crisis and Challenge - The Test and Overcoming of Leadership

Chapter 1: Crisis Management

1.1 Strategic Response in the Battle of Red Cliff: Lessons in Crisis Management from *The Three Kingdoms*

The Battle of Red Cliff is one of the most renowned battles in *The Three Kingdoms*, often cited as a classic case of overcoming crisis. At that time, Cao Cao led an army of 800,000 troops from the north to attack Liu Bei and Sun Quan in the south. Although Cao Cao's forces were overwhelming, the allied forces of Liu Bei and Sun Quan were severely lacking in troops and resources. This battle provides a valuable lesson on how to survive and achieve victory despite facing overwhelming odds, making it a remarkable example for leaders in strategizing their response to crisis situations.

One of the key lessons from the Battle of Red Cliff is the importance of thorough information analysis and the ability to identify the enemy's weaknesses. Zhuge Liang and Zhou Yu noted that, while Cao Cao's massive army was powerful, it was inexperienced in naval warfare. Cao Cao's troops were primarily trained for land-based combat, and, after a long expedition, morale among his soldiers was low. Furthermore, disease was spreading within his ranks. Zhuge Liang and Zhou Yu saw that despite the intimidating size of Cao Cao's army, it was internally vulnerable, and they used this insight to develop a strategic response.

In today's business environment, identifying a competitor's weaknesses in response to market changes or crisis situations is essential. For instance, if competitors rely heavily on specific technology or operate in limited markets, a strategy can be devised to exploit those weaknesses. In this era of digital transformation, some companies struggle with innovation due to rigid adherence to traditional business models, while others quickly capitalize on such gaps to dominate the market. As in the Battle of Red Cliff, information analysis and pinpointing vulnerabilities are critical to gaining a competitive edge.

The strategy Zhuge Liang and Zhou Yu implemented by using fire and wind to attack Cao Cao's army demonstrates creative problem-solving. They utilized the natural wind direction to launch an unexpected and innovative fire attack on Cao Cao's forces, causing significant confusion and disruption. By opting for an unconventional strategy, Zhuge Liang and Zhou Yu overcame a dangerous crisis with creativity.

Similarly, in modern business management, creative thinking is crucial in times of crisis. Particularly in rapidly changing market environments, innovative problem-solving is often required to overcome obstacles. For example, Uber transformed the traditional taxi industry by introducing a mobile app-based vehicle-calling service, creating a new market space. When many believed that transforming the taxi industry would be difficult, Uber's creative solution revolutionized the global transportation system. Zhuge Liang and Zhou Yu's inventive strategies serve as an inspiration for today's leaders.

Another lesson from the Battle of Red Cliff is the power of alliances and collaboration. Liu Bei and Sun Quan formed a coalition to face Cao Cao's army. This alliance was mutually complementary, with Sun Quan's naval forces and Liu Bei's land forces working together to defeat Cao Cao's army. A crucial aspect of this collaboration was understanding each party's strengths and weaknesses to create a complementary strategy.

In times of crisis, leaders must not overlook the importance of collaboration. Partnerships with external allies can often be a breakthrough in overcoming crises. For instance, Tesla collaborated with Panasonic to accelerate growth in the electric vehicle industry. Panasonic's battery technology significantly supported Tesla's leadership in the electric vehicle market. In crisis situations, mutual collaboration becomes a powerful force.

Finally, the Battle of Red Cliff teaches the importance of decisiveness and drive in leadership. Despite the overwhelming strength of Cao Cao's army, Liu Bei and Sun Quan made bold decisions. Liu Bei avoided direct confrontation with Cao Cao through collaboration with Zhuge Liang and chose a long-term strategic alliance with Sun Quan. This decision did not focus on short-term victory but was aligned with a long-term vision, ultimately playing a key role in his dream of unifying *The Three Kingdoms*.

Decisiveness in leadership is just as crucial in modern management. Without bold decision-making in times of crisis, organizations may quickly fall into chaos. For example, companies that recognize the need for digital transformation but fail to act on it risk falling behind their competitors. Kodak, which was aware of digital camera technology but did not adopt it aggressively, was ultimately left behind, leading to bankruptcy. On the other hand, Netflix achieved remarkable growth by boldly shifting to streaming services, positioning itself as a leader in the global media industry.

The Battle of Red Cliff is an exemplary case of crisis management, combining thorough information analysis, creative thinking, the importance of collaboration, and decisive leadership.

1.2 Overcoming Crisis in the Battle of Myeongnyang: Strategic Decisions by Admiral Yi Sun-sin

The Battle of Myeongnyang is considered one of the most remarkable naval battles in Korean history, often cited as a model for overcoming crises. At that time, Admiral Yi Sun-sin faced the daunting challenge of defending against a Japanese fleet with just 12 ships against their 330. Despite these dire circumstances, Admiral Yi maintained a calm assessment of the battle situation, exercised exceptional judgment, and led his forces to victory. This battle serves as a defining example of leadership and crisis management.

The first lesson from the Battle of Myeongnyang is the importance of courage and decisiveness. Before the battle began, Admiral Yi famously said, "I still have 12 ships left," instilling courage in his soldiers and demonstrating his unwavering resolve to fight to the end. This moment marked an important instance where he showed his conviction as a leader, inspiring confidence in his men. Motivated by Admiral Yi's decisiveness, his soldiers resolved to face the vastly superior enemy fleet.

In times of crisis, leaders need to show courage and decisiveness. Particularly when an organization faces serious challenges, hesitation or fear from a leader can lead to further instability and confusion. For example, during the 2008 global financial crisis, Toyota made the bold decision to downsize production lines. Though this decision risked short-term losses, it ultimately became a crucial strategic choice for recovery. Like Admiral Yi, leaders' courageous decisions are essential for steering organizations through crises.

The second lesson is the efficient use of resources. Admiral Yi made strategic use of the narrow straits in Myeongnyang, using the bottlenecked geography to his advantage. By limiting the Japanese fleet's mobility and confining them to a single position, he was able to neutralize the enemy's numerical superiority and destroy them sequentially. This demonstrates a model strategy for maximizing limited resources effectively.

Resource efficiency is also indispensable in modern management. Particularly for startups or small businesses with limited resources, strategies that maximize resource efficiency are essential. For instance, using low-cost, high-impact strategies such as social media marketing allows companies with limited budgets to reach their target market effectively. Such resource efficiency is essential to maintaining competitiveness in challenging times.

The third lesson is the value of trust among subordinates. Admiral Yi's soldiers trusted him completely, which gave them the strength to fight to the end in a seemingly hopeless situation. Yi constantly communicated with his men, clearly explaining why and how they had to fight. Through this, his soldiers placed their full confidence in his leadership and were prepared to fight with their lives on the line.

Similarly, leaders must build trust within their organizations. In crises, transparent and honest communication is necessary so that team members can trust their leaders. Steve Jobs, for instance, built trust with his team at Apple through open communication, and, as a result, his employees stood by him during challenging times. Such trust provides the foundation for organizations to unite and deliver results, even in times of crisis.

Finally, a long-term vision is crucial. Admiral Yi's purpose extended beyond simply winning battles; he was driven by the long-term vision of protecting his homeland. This vision fueled his courage and decisiveness. After the Battle of Myeongnyang, Admiral Yi continued to prepare for further Japanese attacks by developing a long-term strategy, underscoring the importance of leadership that looks beyond immediate problems and prepares for the future.

Leaders, too, should go beyond merely overcoming short-term crises and lead with a long-term vision and goals. Jeff Bezos, in Amazon's early days, prioritized long-term growth over short-term profits by making bold investments, which ultimately enabled Amazon to grow into the global powerhouse it is today. A long-term strategy and vision, as demonstrated by Admiral Yi, are essential to sustainable growth in any organization.

The courage, decisiveness, efficient resource management, trust-building, and long-term vision demonstrated by Admiral Yi in the Battle of Myeongnyang are critical leadership lessons for overcoming crises and leading organizations to success in modern business management.

Chapter 2: Decision-Making and Responsibility

2.1. The Importance of Decisiveness: Lessons from Romance of *The Three Kingdoms* and Admiral Yi Sun-sin

In leadership, decisiveness is an essential virtue. It means not only making swift decisions but also the ability to carefully assess various factors in complex situations and make the optimal choice.

Examples from Romance of *The Three Kingdoms* and the life of Admiral Yi Sun-sin illustrate how decisiveness is a crucial element that can make or break a leader's success. Leaders must analyze information thoroughly, anticipate potential outcomes, and make bold and prompt decisions.

In Romance of *The Three Kingdoms*, Liu Bei frequently demonstrated decisiveness. Notably, during the Battle of Red Cliffs, he had to decide whether to form an alliance with Sun Quan to confront Cao Cao's overwhelming forces or to retreat to ensure his safety. By accepting Zhuge Liang's advice and choosing to ally, Liu Bei successfully countered Cao Cao's army, which became a pivotal moment in expanding his influence within the events of *The Three Kingdoms*. Without this decision, Liu Bei would likely have faced defeat, upsetting the balance of *The Three Kingdoms*.

This kind of decisiveness is an essential attribute for modern leaders who seek success.

Admiral Yi Sun-sin and the Battle of Hansando: Another Lesson in Decisiveness

Admiral Yi Sun-sin's victory at the Battle of Hansando demonstrates another valuable lesson in decisiveness. This naval battle, which took place in 1592 during the Imjin War (Japanese invasions of Korea), required Admiral Yi to devise a critical strategy to halt the advancing Japanese forces. He recognized the numerical superiority of the Japanese fleet but analyzed the advantages of the terrain and the enemy's tactical weaknesses, leading him to make the decision to lure the enemy fleet into the waters off Hansando Island.

Yi capitalized on the narrow straits of Hansando, dispersing the Japanese fleet and employing the "crane-wing formation" to encircle them. This decision, based on strategic judgment rather than yielding to the enemy's superior numbers, resulted in an overwhelming victory for the Korean navy and significantly weakened Japan's naval strength.

This demonstration of decisiveness highlights how a calm, optimal choice can lead to substantial results. Had he hesitated or chosen to retreat, Korea's naval strength would have suffered, and preventing Japan's advance would have been much more challenging.

Liu Bei's Decisiveness: Establishing the Kingdom of Shu Han and His Long-term Strategy

Another example of Liu Bei's decisiveness is found in his decision to establish the Kingdom of Shu Han. After losing Jingzhou and facing difficulties with his alliance with Sun Quan, Liu Bei saw an opportunity to move westward to Yizhou to establish a new base. Although Yizhou presented high risks due to its remoteness and the existing power of Wei and Wu, he recognized that without new endeavors, his forces would have little chance of survival.

Despite concerns from generals Zhang Fei and Guan Yu, Liu Bei moved forward decisively. He relied on his leadership and Zhuge Liang's strategic advice to push into Yizhou, eventually creating the foundation for the Kingdom of Shu and maintaining a balance between *The Three Kingdoms*. This example illustrates how leaders can succeed in uncertain situations by making strategic decisions with a long-term vision and accepting risks.

In modern management, taking risks when making decisions is important because successful leadership requires leaders not only to prioritize safe choices but, at times, to make choices that embrace risk to ensure long-term success. Liu Bei's decision to advance into Yizhou exemplifies how his leadership and decisiveness contributed to Shu Han's growth.

The Need for Decisiveness in Modern Management

Decisiveness remains a critical skill for leaders today. In today's rapidly changing business landscape, leaders often face situations where they must make critical decisions. Whether facing a crisis or considering a new opportunity, decisiveness is a key factor that often separates successful leaders from unsuccessful ones. A leader must be able to make timely decisions based on accurate information to set the organization's course.

Furthermore, future-focused insights and data-driven decision-making can aid leaders in making the best choices in uncertain environments.

For instance, Netflix, anticipating future market trends, took the decisive step to shift from its DVD rental business to streaming services, pivoting boldly to a digital content business model. Although this choice involved considerable risk at the time, it has led to Netflix's global success today.

When leaders make decisions, risk is an inherent part of the process. However, the core of leadership is having the courage to take bold action and to steer toward success by taking responsibility for the outcome.

Decisiveness and Responsibility: Essential Traits for Leaders

Ultimately, decisiveness is closely linked to responsibility in leadership. Leaders who act decisively determine the direction of the organization and must take responsibility for the outcomes. This entails not only making decisions that will likely lead to success but also facing potential failure with courage and accountability.

Liu Bei and Admiral Yi Sun-sin accepted full responsibility for their decisions, one of the key reasons they are remembered as exemplary leaders. Modern executives must also show the courage to make bold decisions in times of crisis and the strength to lead the organization toward future success. Additionally, they must have the integrity to accept responsibility for the results of their decisions, no matter the outcome, and continue guiding the organization forward.

2.2. Responsibility: The Duty and Attitude of a Leader

In leadership, decisiveness is crucial, but so is responsibility, which is a core virtue that leaders must possess. Since leaders set the organization's direction, they must take responsibility for the outcomes of all their decisions. Ultimately, an organization's success or failure stems from the leader's decisions, and therefore, a sense of responsibility profoundly influences both the leader's trustworthiness and the organization's sustainability.

When leaders demonstrate a sense of responsibility, the weight of their decisions becomes evident, and followers are more likely to trust and follow them. This sense of responsibility includes not only owning positive outcomes but also accepting accountability for failed decisions. Leaders should take full responsibility for their decisions and their consequences, and this responsible attitude plays a significant role in fostering trust and successful organization management.

Liu Bei in Romance of *The Three Kingdoms*: A Lesson in Responsible Leadership

In Romance of *The Three Kingdoms*, Liu Bei frequently displayed responsible leadership. He took ownership of his decisions during critical moments without shifting blame onto his subordinates, even when he had made mistakes. This sense of responsibility was one of the key reasons his followers deeply trusted him.

When Liu Bei lost Jingzhou, he did not attribute this loss to his subordinates or circumstances but accepted it as a mistake in his own judgment, specifically in miscalculating his alliance with Sun Quan. By taking responsibility, Liu Bei strengthened the loyalty and trust of his followers, which became the foundation of his leadership.

Throughout his leadership, Liu Bei strove to build trust within his organization, where his responsibility-based leadership was crucial. He protected his followers even when they made mistakes, assuming full responsibility as a leader. This sense of responsibility contributed significantly to his followers' devotion and loyalty. Liu Bei's leadership is an excellent example of how leaders can foster trust in an organization through a sense of responsibility.

Admiral Yi Sun-sin:
A Symbol of Responsibility and Dedication

Admiral Yi Sun-sin is an emblematic figure of responsible leadership. He took full responsibility for every decision he made in battle, regardless of the outcome, consistently bearing the consequences himself. This sense of responsibility was one of the major reasons his subordinates had unwavering trust in him.
Admiral Yi led with a commitment to take responsibility first. For example, after the Battle of Chilcheollyang, where Won Gyun was defeated, and the Korean navy suffered devastating losses, Admiral Yi did not blame the situation or assign responsibility to others. Instead, he took charge of rebuilding the navy and devoted himself to re-establishing his forces. This demonstrated the importance of responsibility not only in warfare but also in the process of rebuilding an organization.

His dedication was evident in his constant preparation, regardless of the situation. Even after victories, Admiral Yi remained humble and continued rigorous preparations for future battles. This attitude of responsibility earned the trust of his subordinates, who were willing to follow him wholeheartedly, even at the cost of their own lives.

Admiral Yi's responsible leadership is why he is remembered as a respected historical leader, and his example of responsibility is still a crucial quality for modern leaders.

**Responsibility in Modern Management:
A Leader's Response to Failed Decisions**

In modern management, responsible leadership is also a critical virtue. Leaders should be prepared not only to take responsibility for success but also to accept accountability for failed decisions. When leaders acknowledge their mistakes and work towards solutions, they build trust within the organization, which enhances their credibility as leaders.

Satya Nadella of Microsoft is a notable example of responsible leadership. After Microsoft's acquisition of Nokia led to substantial losses, Nadella did not evade responsibility. Instead, he acknowledged the mistake under his leadership and focused on resetting the company's strategy. He accepted the loss from the Nokia acquisition, implemented plans to stabilize the company, and formulated a new growth strategy.

Responsible leadership, therefore, plays an essential role in learning from failures and creating growth opportunities. When leaders take responsibility for failed decisions and find solutions, they provide the organization with an opportunity to move in a new direction. This demonstrates how leaders can grow an organization and sustain trust through accountability.

The Impact of Responsible Leadership on an Organization

A responsible leader should not fear failure but view it as a learning opportunity for future preparation. This leads not only to problem-solving but also to leadership aimed at long-term success, which fosters growth opportunities for the future.

By embracing responsibility, leaders build trust within the organization and create an environment where members feel empowered to take risks without fear of failure.

Responsibility also significantly affects organizational morale and performance. When leaders avoid responsibility or shift blame onto subordinates, trust within the organization deteriorates, and members lose loyalty toward the leader. However, when leaders assume responsibility and act decisively, members develop respect for the leader, motivating them to fulfill their roles more faithfully.

Furthermore, responsible leaders can turn failure into an

opportunity, making better decisions that lay the groundwork for growth and innovation. This process of learning from failure and leading toward success has a positive impact on the entire organization, strengthening trust between the leader and the members.

Part 4: Success and Failure — The True Value of Leadership

Chapter 1: Learning from Failure

1.1. Liu Bei's Failures and Comebacks: Lessons on Failure from Romance of *The Three Kingdoms*

In Romance of *The Three Kingdoms*, Liu Bei is a prime example of someone who experienced numerous failures and setbacks, yet overcame them to achieve success. Unlike other rulers, he did not start with a strong military force or a solid political foundation. Rather, Liu Bei began with minimal resources and built his power incrementally, learning valuable lessons from each failure along the way.

Liu Bei's growth into a central figure in *The Three Kingdoms* era demonstrates that failure need not be the end but can be a valuable opportunity for growth. His journey serves as a lesson to leaders that they should not fear failure but view it as a means of improvement.

Liu Bei's early defeats included both military failures and political betrayals. Time and again, he clashed with Cao Cao, a far more powerful adversary, and was often defeated by Cao Cao's overwhelming military strength. As Cao Cao commanded both military and political dominance, Liu Bei frequently suffered defeats, even at times leading a fugitive's life on the run. He lost loyal followers, faced danger to his family, and yet never stopped seeking paths to rebuild.

Through these experiences, Liu Bei came to understand his own weaknesses and considered how best to compensate for them.

One of Liu Bei's first major failures occurred during his conflicts with Cao Cao, whose formidable northern forces repeatedly overpowered him. Fleeing from Cao Cao, Liu Bei became acutely aware of his vulnerabilities, recognizing not only his lack of military power but also his limitations in strategic thinking and his weak political base. From this failure, he learned the importance of recruiting strategic talent.

The Loss of Jing Province: Liu Bei's Setback and Lesson Learned

Liu Bei's failures extended beyond military defeats to include political betrayal and the collapse of alliances. Losing Jing Province was one of the greatest setbacks of his life. Jing Province was a crucial military and political stronghold for Liu Bei, obtained through his alliance with Sun Quan. However, when he lost the province following Guan Yu's defeat, Liu Bei incurred a significant political blow.

The loss of Jing Province taught Liu Bei the importance of alliances and the challenges of maintaining political balance. Sun Quan's betrayal and the end of their alliance highlighted the need for Liu Bei to manage and sustain his alliances more cautiously.

This experience provides an essential lesson for modern leaders: partnerships and alliances are critical to success, yet their maintenance and careful management are crucial, as shown by Liu Bei's experience.

Leadership Through Learning from Failure

Although Liu Bei's life was filled with failures and setbacks, he never considered these events mere defeats. Instead, he drew important lessons from his failures and used them as stepping stones for recovery. Recognizing his strategic weaknesses, he poured effort into recruiting Zhuge Liang (also known as Zhuge Kongming). Understanding that he needed Zhuge Liang's wisdom and expertise, Liu Bei visited him three times in his quest to enlist his support. This dedication illustrates the importance for leaders to recognize their own limitations and seek out the right individuals to complement them.

With Zhuge Liang on his team, Liu Bei compensated for his lack of strategic expertise, gaining greater confidence in his decisions.

This lesson holds true in modern business as well.

Leaders must be aware of their strengths and weaknesses and complement their limitations by recruiting the right talent and building a team. Liu Bei's leadership emphasizes the importance of humility and continuous learning, underscoring that hiring the right people for the right roles is essential in achieving success in today's business landscape.

Using Failure as a Springboard for Revival: Liu Bei's Persistence and Patience

Liu Bei never regarded failure as mere defeat. Instead, he constantly sought new opportunities, refusing to give up and always exploring ways to rebound. His persistence and patience ultimately led him to become the Emperor of Shu Han, marking a pivotal moment in the history of *The Three Kingdoms*.

Liu Bei's resilience went beyond merely overcoming defeat, playing a critical role in his ability to transform failure into new opportunities. Modern leaders must also use persistence and patience to find growth opportunities in the face of failure. Failure should be viewed not as an end but as a chance to try again, uncovering new possibilities. Liu Bei demonstrated this by learning from his setbacks and subsequently reorganizing his strategies and leadership.

The Lesson of Failure in Modern Management: How to Turn It into Growth

Modern leaders, too, need to see failure as an opportunity for growth. Founders of startups often encounter failure in the early stages due to funding issues, lack of market response, or technical limitations. However, these failures can provide valuable lessons that help them better understand market needs and prepare for renewed attempts.

For example, when Uber first launched, it faced regulatory and legal issues in many cities, temporarily halting its services. Though this might seem like an early failure, Uber responded by thoroughly analyzing each city's legal requirements and developing strategies to relaunch successfully. Uber's experience demonstrates the importance of not fearing failure but rather finding new opportunities within it.

Ultimately, leaders must approach failure as a chance for growth and use it to guide their organization's development. Liu Bei's ability to identify new possibilities within failure and transform them into success offers a valuable lesson for today's leaders.

1.2. The Failures and Comebacks of Admiral Yi Sun-sin: The Power of Leadership That Saved a Nation

Admiral Yi Sun-sin is revered as one of the greatest military leaders in Korean history, yet his life was filled with trials marked by numerous failures and setbacks. His demotion and the unjust slander he endured placed him in a position not only as a military leader but as a figure who continually rose from failure, embodying resilience as a leader.

Through Admiral Yi's journey of setbacks and comebacks, leaders today can glean valuable lessons on how to turn failure into a stepping stone for recovery and growth.

Unjust Demotion and Wrongful Accusations: Admiral Yi's Setbacks

Despite Admiral Yi's series of victories during the Japanese invasions of Korea (Imjin War), he faced demotion due to political schemes and power struggles. Following his successive triumphs over the Japanese forces, Yi Sun-sin found himself stripped of all military authority and imprisoned due to political attacks and slander. This situation not only risked undoing his battlefield achievements but also tested his conviction as a leader.

Even while imprisoned, Admiral Yi did not fixate on political schemes or personal reputation. Instead, he prepared himself for the day he could once again defend his country and people. By enduring unjust treatment and refusing to yield to political pressure, Yi Sun-sin exhibited a strong will to fulfill his duty. His unwavering commitment was not only an example of his leadership as a military commander but also underscored his dedication and responsibility as a leader.

The reason Admiral Yi was able to uphold his beliefs through such trials lay in his sense of duty to protect his nation. Without concern for personal honor or position, he carried on with loyalty and accountability to overcome setbacks. This example highlights for today's leaders how to preserve their vision and guide their organization through difficult times.

Modern leaders facing challenges that jeopardize trust due to internal political pressures or external factors should follow Admiral Yi's example by consistently upholding and conveying their goals and vision.

The Defeat at the Battle of Chilcheollyang and Lessons Learned

The Battle of Chilcheollyang was a devastating defeat for the Korean Navy that occurred after Admiral Yi's demotion and absence. During this period, Won Gyun was in command of the Korean fleet, but due to poor strategic judgment and inadequate preparation, the Korean Navy suffered nearly complete destruction. This defeat dealt a catastrophic blow to Korea's naval power.

For Admiral Yi, this defeat came with heavy responsibility and pressure, yet he did not view it merely as a setback but rather as a foundation for recovery. The court once again entrusted him with command, and he devoted himself to rebuilding the navy. Yi Sun-sin absorbed the lessons of this defeat, using it as a foundation to formulate new strategies and prepare for battle once more.

Admiral Yi did not allow the loss at Chilcheollyang to remain a tragedy of the past. Instead, he took this defeat as an opportunity to rebuild the navy and reform his tactics, rigorously preparing to achieve better results in future battles.

This process of recovery offers critical insights for modern leaders as well. Failure should be seen as an opportunity for growth. Leaders must analyze the causes of failure and apply strategic thinking to prepare for future success.

Relentless Preparation for Revival:
Admiral Yi's Leadership

The reason Admiral Yi was able to overcome setbacks and failures and return to lead was due to his unceasing preparation and sense of responsibility. He firmly believed that the day would come when he would have to fight again and continued studying tactics and strategies. Even while demoted, he kept an eye on the navy's state, made strategic adjustments as needed, and prepared to return to the battlefield at any moment.

Admiral Yi's successful comeback can be attributed to his ability to learn from failure and transform those lessons into a growth opportunity through thorough preparation. He did not merely resign himself to defeat but instead continued to refine his strategic thinking to prepare for the next battle.

This attitude from Admiral Yi provides modern leaders with valuable guidance. Even after failure, leaders should continuously learn, prepare for a comeback, and persist in searching for new strategies.

Admiral Yi's Sense of Responsibility: Leadership for the Nation

Admiral Yi consistently emphasized his responsibility to fulfill his role. Regardless of the outcome of battles, he maintained a steadfast attitude to assume full responsibility. Even when demoted due to political schemes, he did not abandon his mission to protect the nation, holding onto the day he could fulfill his duty.

This sense of responsibility was central to Admiral Yi's leadership and was a driving force in his ability to overcome setbacks. Through this responsible leadership, he earned the absolute trust of his subordinates, and when the opportunity to return to the battlefield arose, his soldiers were willing to follow him with unwavering loyalty.

There is much for modern leaders to learn from Admiral Yi's example of responsibility. Leaders must have the resolve to assume complete responsibility for both the successes and failures of their organizations. In recognizing and learning from failure, they can restore trust within their organization.

Admiral Yi's actions demonstrated that failure need not be a permanent setback but instead can become a renewed opportunity. This lesson in leadership offers a deep source of inspiration for modern management.

Turning Failure into a Growth Opportunity

The setbacks and failures of Admiral Yi ultimately transformed him into a stronger leader. Despite political betrayal and unjust demotion, he reaffirmed his mission and seized the opportunity for a comeback.

Modern leaders can gain valuable lessons from Admiral Yi's journey through failure and revival. Failure should not be seen as a moment of defeat but as a foundation for greater growth. By analyzing the causes of failure and learning from them, leaders can prepare for future success.

Just as Admiral Yi continually learned and grew even after setbacks, modern leaders must maintain strategic thinking to overcome failure and lead their organizations through continuous learning and effort.

Chapter 2: Humble Leadership

2.1. Liu Bei's Humble Leadership: A Commitment to Lifelong Learning, Even in Success

Liu Bei established his position as a successful ruler in *The Three Kingdoms*, but what made him a truly exemplary leader was his unwavering humility, even after achieving success.

While many rulers become dictatorial or arrogant after gaining power, ignoring the counsel of those around them, Liu Bei retained a humble attitude even after ascending as Emperor of Shu-Han. He recognized his own shortcomings, listened to his subordinates, and emphasized the importance of cooperation. This humility in Liu Bei's leadership was a significant reason why he continued to earn the trust of his subordinates and why they remained loyal to him until the end.

The Essence of Humble Leadership: Learning from Subordinates

After attaining success and becoming the Emperor of Shu-Han, Liu Bei did not consider his achievements as his own alone. Instead, he consistently acknowledged his limitations and celebrated the contributions of his subordinates. Liu Bei collaborated with talented figures such as Zhuge Liang, Guan Yu, and Zhang Fei, drawing on their wisdom and experience to make better decisions.

This humility enabled him to continue growing as a leader committed to learning.

Liu Bei's relationship with Zhuge Liang particularly underscored his willingness to learn. He regarded Zhuge Liang as a mentor, constantly seeking his advice and respecting his opinions when making strategic decisions. Through this approach of learning from subordinates, Liu Bei complemented his own judgment and achieved better outcomes through cooperation.

For today's leaders, this provides an important lesson: even for a successful leader, staying open to learning and accepting the perspectives of those around them is crucial for sustainable leadership.

The Importance of Humble Leadership: Lessons from Liu Bei's Leadership

Liu Bei's humble leadership was a key reason he continued to grow, even after his successes. Upon founding Shu-Han and becoming Emperor, he continued to reflect on his decisions, listen to the opinions of his subordinates, and remain open to learning.

While many leaders tend to become authoritarian after success, or resist change by clinging to their methods, Liu Bei humbly acknowledged that his success was the result of collaboration with his subordinates. In particular, his leadership emphasized recognizing the achievements of his subordinates and working with them humbly. After winning battles, Liu Bei didn't monopolize the credit but respected the roles of his subordinates and shared the honors with them. His humility played an essential role in securing his long-term success as a respected ruler.

In modern management, humble leadership plays a vital role in an organization's success. When a leader is fixated on their methods and refuses to listen to others, an organization can eventually hit a growth ceiling.

Humble Leadership in Modern Management:
The Importance of Continuous Learning After Success

In modern business, humble leadership is recognized as a critical virtue, especially in fast-changing markets. Rather than becoming complacent in their methods, successful leaders can achieve sustainable success by remaining adaptable and committed to continuous learning. Market dynamics are constantly shifting, and to keep up with advances in technology and changes in consumer trends, a flexible leadership approach and a commitment to learning are essential.

For instance, Larry Page, co-founder of Google, continued learning new technologies even after achieving success, always striving to steer the company toward better outcomes. He went beyond the already successful search engine model and invested in research and development of future technologies, such as artificial intelligence, to keep

Google innovating. Google's establishment as a global leader was possible because Larry Page maintained a humble approach to leadership, never content with past success and always pursuing new technologies and challenges.

Much like Liu Bei's humble leadership, modern leaders should never cease to learn, even after success, and should continually strive for sustainable growth. In today's rapidly changing market environment, leaders need to be ready to adapt to new shifts, embrace the wisdom around them, and maintain a mindset of ongoing learning.

The Positive Impact of Humble Leadership on Organizations: Building Trust and Respect

Liu Bei's humble leadership was not simply a personal virtue; it was a quality that made him a highly respected leader among his subordinates. Liu Bei acknowledged his limitations and always honored the contributions of his subordinates.

Whenever he won a battle, he shared the achievements with his team, emphasizing their role. Such humble leadership solidified Liu Bei's trustworthiness in the eyes of his subordinates, who in turn respected and followed him even more closely.

In modern management, a leader's humility plays an essential role in building organizational trust. When a leader acknowledges their limitations, fairly recognizes team contributions, and listens to members' opinions, trust within the organization is strengthened, fostering a positive organizational culture.

On the other hand, if a leader clings only to their approach and disregards others' contributions, members may lose motivation and be less inclined to contribute to the organization's growth.

Liu Bei's humble leadership highlights the importance of trust and cooperation for organizational success. He not only refused to claim success as his own but always emphasized the achievements of his team and worked with them collaboratively. This approach to leadership made him a long-term successful ruler respected by his followers, offering valuable lessons for leaders today.

Leaders Who Share Success: Building Trust with Team Members

Modern leaders should also learn that achieving success alone isn't enough; sharing successes with team members and recognizing their contributions is crucial for building trust within an organization.

Through his leadership, Liu Bei ensured that the rewards of success were shared across the organization, fostering respect and trust in his leadership among his team members. Such humble leadership contributed to creating a positive culture within the organization, where members respected and willingly followed their leader.

In modern management, a humble leader can strengthen trust with team members and maximize the organization's overall success. When leaders share achievements and acknowledge contributions, organizations achieve sustained growth, and members gain motivation to produce even greater results.

2.2. Admiral Yi Sun-sin's Humble Leadership: A Commitment to Lifelong Learning

Admiral Yi Sun-sin achieved numerous strategic victories, but his true leadership went far beyond mere military ability. His greatest strength was his humility, which he maintained even in moments of victory, never boasting but instead embodying humble leadership until the end.

He consistently recognized his soldiers' contributions and shared in the joy of victory with them. Admiral Yi frequently expressed gratitude to his men, and his humility and leadership inspired their unwavering trust. This form of humble leadership offers a valuable lesson not only in times of war but also in modern management.

Building Trust Through Humble Leadership with Soldiers

Although Admiral Yi earned many victories, he never regarded these achievements as solely his own. Instead, he consistently valued the contributions of his soldiers and demonstrated heartfelt gratitude for their efforts. After major victories, he refrained from emphasizing his own abilities and instead credited his soldiers' bravery and sacrifices, acknowledging that victory would have been impossible without them. This approach to leadership earned him the respect and loyalty of his troops.

Admiral Yi also maintained humility in his communication with subordinates. When planning military strategies, he would discuss his ideas with them and listen to their advice. This wasn't merely about enforcing orders; it was about creating an environment where soldiers could prepare alongside their leader and take ownership of their roles. By establishing an environment where subordinates felt free to share their opinions, Admiral Yi strengthened mutual trust and motivated them to follow him in battle.

A humble leader plays a critical role in fostering organizational trust by genuinely recognizing subordinates' contributions and sharing their achievements throughout the organization. Admiral Yi's humble leadership solidified his role as a respected leader and offers valuable lessons for modern leaders. When leaders acknowledge the contributions of their team and express gratitude, they build a foundation of trust within the organization, and team members gain a deeper sense of responsibility and pride in their roles.

A Leader's Endless Pursuit of Knowledge: Admiral Yi's Commitment to Lifelong Learning

Admiral Yi was not only humble but was also a lifelong learner, always striving to improve. Despite his numerous victories, he never allowed himself to rest on his successes.

Admiral Yi continued to study new strategies and tactics, always preparing for the next battle without becoming complacent. He analyzed battle outcomes, examined enemy movements, and constantly strategized on how to fight more effectively. This ongoing commitment to learning was one of the key reasons behind his consistent victories.

He deeply studied naval tactics, adjusted his strategies to align with enemy movements, and analyzed mistakes and areas for improvement even after victories, further refining his leadership. This attitude of humble learning offers a valuable lesson to today's business leaders.

Leaders must continuously pursue learning, even after success, and remain prepared for new challenges. Rather than settling for past accomplishments, leaders who seek new learning opportunities and strive for better outcomes are needed.

In modern business, Admiral Yi's dedication to lifelong learning shows the essential qualities that leaders need to foster long-term growth within an organization. Successful leaders, as Admiral Yi demonstrated, must be willing to learn more and self-reflect to drive the organization forward.

For instance, Satya Nadella, CEO of Microsoft, exemplified this attitude by continuously embracing new technology and innovation. Through open communication with employees, he listened to all perspectives and led Microsoft to become a global leader once again. This shows how an enduring commitment to learning is essential for the long-term success of an organization.

Through his battle experience, Admiral Yi constantly learned, refined his strategies, and demonstrated humility. He never let success intoxicate him but instead prepared tirelessly for future challenges. This attitude of continuous learning offers modern leaders critical insight into what it takes to continue growing after achieving success.

A Commitment to Fulfilling Responsibilities: Humility and Learning Combined

Admiral Yi's humble leadership did not stop at mere virtue; it extended to a commitment to fulfilling his duties until the end. He firmly believed that defending his country was his mission, and he carried out this responsibility until the very end.

No matter the crisis, he never retreated but led his forces

with determination. Admiral Yi did not avoid his responsibilities as a leader. He made decisions based on a deep sense of duty and dedicated himself fully to his country.

Modern business leaders have much to learn from Admiral Yi's leadership. Leaders should recognize that success and failure are collective achievements and maintain a commitment to their responsibilities until the end.

Leadership that shares success with team members and acknowledges their contributions is essential for building trust and respect within an organization. When leaders remain humble after success and continue learning, they pave the way for sustained organizational growth.

Admiral Yi's humble leadership earned him trust and respect through lifelong learning and dedication. Today's leaders can guide their organizations to success by embodying similar humility. Humility is not just a virtue; it is a cornerstone of respected leadership that earns loyalty from team members.

Lessons for Modern Management: The Importance of Lifelong Learning in Leadership

Admiral Yi's humble, knowledge-seeking leadership offers valuable lessons for modern business. Leaders must continue learning, even after success, and remain prepared for new challenges. Rather than becoming complacent with past achievements, they should be adaptable to change and open to the wisdom around them, leading to long-term organizational success.

Modern leaders like Satya Nadella, inspired by Admiral Yi's leadership, continue to maintain a commitment to learning after success, always pursuing new opportunities. Admiral Yi's humble leadership, marked by lifelong learning and a dedication to responsibility, serves as a powerful inspiration for leaders seeking to make a meaningful impact in today's world.

Part 5: Preparing for the Future - Innovation and Sustainability

Chapter 1: Flexible Leadership

1.1 Sun Quan's Strategic Adaptability and Flexibility: Leadership Suited to Circumstances

In *The Romance of The Three Kingdoms*, Sun Quan is portrayed as a unique and adaptable leader. Unlike Liu Bei or Cao Cao, he did not possess a powerful military background but was able to maintain his country's stability over a long period by changing strategies based on external situations and responding with flexibility. This leadership style provides valuable lessons for today's leaders in adapting to shifting markets and business environments.

Sun Quan's Strategic Flexibility: Responding Swiftly to External Situations
One of Sun Quan's key strengths was his ability to respond swiftly to external situations. As the ruler of Wu in the south, he faced the complex situation of balancing between the powerful adversaries Cao Cao and Liu Bei. By sometimes aligning with Liu Bei and other times with Cao Cao, Sun Quan effectively maintained his power by adjusting strategies to fit the situation. Such flexibility allowed Wu to remain a formidable force during the turbu-

lent Three Kingdoms period.

The first major lesson from Sun Quan's leadership is "strategic flexibility." Sun Quan recognized Wu's relatively weaker military power and compensated by skillfully leveraging external alliances. For example, after allying with Liu Bei to defeat Cao Cao's forces at the Battle of Red Cliffs, Sun Quan later readjusted his relationship with Liu Bei based on changing circumstances. This kind of strategic flexibility is essential for today's leaders to survive in constantly changing business environments.

The Importance of Flexible Leadership in Modern Management

In today's business world, external environments are in constant flux due to technological advancements, economic shifts, and political instability. Flexible leadership is essential for adapting to these changes.

Apple, for instance, began as a computer company but quickly entered the mobile device market with the iPhone and iPad, achieving tremendous success. Apple's ability to swiftly adapt to market shifts and embrace technological innovation is a notable example of flexible strategy akin to Sun Quan's leadership. This shows that leaders must be ready to adjust strategies promptly to navigate the challenges of an ever-changing market and environment.

The Importance of External Cooperation: Sun Quan's Alliance Strategy

The second key lesson from Sun Quan's leadership is the importance of external cooperation. Realizing that Wu alone could not counter the might of Cao Cao's forces, Sun Quan allied with Liu Bei to achieve a major victory at the Battle of Red Cliffs. By leveraging the alliance, he safeguarded Wu's survival, and this strategy significantly strengthened his position.

In modern business, partnerships and collaborations are also vital to strengthening competitiveness, particularly in global markets. For example, Starbucks has partnered with various global brands to successfully expand its reach internationally. Through a cooperative approach tailored to each region, Starbucks has achieved success worldwide. Just as Sun Quan leveraged alliances strategically, modern leaders must develop partnerships based on market conditions.

Moreover, when forming alliances, Sun Quan made strategic decisions not only with Wu's interests in mind but also considering the broader benefits to his state. This underscores the value of cooperation not merely for short-term gains but for long-term growth.

In a global economy, cooperating with competitors may sometimes be necessary. Sun Quan's ability to navigate alliances with both Liu Bei and Cao Cao reflects the balance between competition and cooperation that leaders must strike.

Flexibility in Internal Organization: Sun Quan's Talent Management

The final lesson from Sun Quan's flexible leadership is the importance of flexibility in internal organization. Sun Quan not only managed external alliances but also fostered an environment where diverse talents could thrive internally.

By appointing the right people to suitable positions, he ensured military and political stability. Leaders like Zhou Yu, Lu Su, and Lü Meng were given important roles and allowed to excel, with Sun Quan entrusting them with authority. This flexibility in talent management is essential for maximizing efficiency and outcomes within an organization.

Flexible management of organizational structures and personnel remains critical in modern management. Successfully adapting to organizational changes and creating environments that enable talent to excel are keys to successful leadership.

For instance, Google fosters collaboration between teams within a flexible work environment that promotes innovation and creativity. Through open communication and a free work culture, Google encourages employees to share creative ideas and achieve innovative outcomes.

Much like Sun Quan, who optimized talent within his organization, today's leaders must be able to quickly adapt to internal changes and maximize the potential of their teams. Flexible organizational management is crucial for achieving long-term success, and Sun Quan's adaptable leadership offers a valuable model for managing internal operations effectively.

The Value of Flexible Leadership

Sun Quan's leadership is a model of adapting strategies to fit both internal and external circumstances. By coordinating competition and cooperation with external forces and efficiently managing talent within, he maintained Wu as a powerful state for an extended period. His leadership illustrates the importance of flexibility in modern management, where leaders must adapt their approach to evolving demands.

Today's leaders must exhibit flexible leadership that can respond to market changes, technological advancements, and economic uncertainties. Sun Quan's leadership transcends time, demonstrating the critical importance of adaptability in leadership.

1.2 Admiral Yi Sun-sin's Strategic Adaptability: Innovative Leadership in Crisis

Admiral Yi Sun-sin is celebrated in Korean history as an exceptional military commander, but his leadership extended beyond battlefield prowess. Yi displayed the ability to adjust his strategies in response to changing wartime conditions and introduced new tactics to adapt to these shifts. His flexible leadership offers valuable lessons for modern leaders on responding innovatively to changing markets and environments.

Strategic Adaptability: Developing Innovative Tactics

A key aspect of Admiral Yi's leadership was his strategic adaptability. During the Japanese invasions of Korea, he introduced the turtle ship—a new weapon equipped with enhanced defenses. The turtle ship's resilience against enemy fire played a pivotal role in naval engagements, providing Korea's navy with a critical advantage against Japan's formidable forces.

Yi also continued to innovate tactically, incorporating the advantages of geographical features to alter battle outcomes. At the Battle of Hansan Island, he used the island's terrain to effectively encircle the Japanese forces, showcasing his flexible and adaptive approach to command. Instead of relying solely on existing tactics, Yi Sun-sin innovated based on battle conditions, successfully repelling Japanese forces.

Lessons for Modern Management: Embracing Innovative Strategies

Today's leaders can learn significant lessons from Admiral Yi's innovative tactics. In a shifting market, clinging to previously successful business models can jeopardize competitiveness. Organizations must actively adopt innovative strategies in response to new situations.

Netflix, for example, began as a DVD rental service but shifted to a streaming model, evolving into a global media leader. Like Yi Sun-sin, Netflix demonstrated the necessity of agile leadership, moving quickly to embrace new strategies and stay ahead of the curve.

Netflix's success underscores the same lesson that Yi's leadership teaches: leaders must adapt swiftly and introduce new strategies to remain competitive.

Effective Resource Utilization: Turning Disadvantages into Advantages

Yi Sun-sin's adaptability was also apparent in his efficient use of resources. Even when facing unfavorable circumstances, he maximized limited resources to achieve decisive victories. At the Battle of Okpo, despite being outnumbered, he capitalized on geographical advantages and his experience in naval warfare to secure a significant win. This strategic use of resources highlights the need for leaders to create effective strategies even when resources are constrained.

Modern leaders frequently encounter resource limitations, especially in competitive markets and during economic downturns. Tesla, for example, navigated early capital constraints and fierce industry competition to establish itself as a leader in electric vehicles by focusing on technological innovation and efficient production. Tesla's approach reflects Yi's ability to manage limited resources strategically, adapting flexibly to situational demands.

Communication and Building Trust: Strong Relationships with Soldiers

An additional lesson from Yi Sun-sin's flexible leadership is the importance of building trust with his soldiers. He prioritized communication and established a foundation of trust, building strong teamwork within his ranks. Yi engaged with his soldiers before battles, clearly explaining strategies and emphasizing the importance of each engagement. This approach fostered loyalty and morale, driving his soldiers to follow him courageously.

Similarly, modern leaders must establish trust to build effective teams. Trust provides a foundation for clearly shared goals and strengthens members' commitment to a leader's decisions.

For example, Jeff Bezos of Amazon communicated a shared vision with employees, ensuring that everyone understood how to respond to changing environments. Like Yi Sun-sin, Bezos built a cohesive organization grounded in trust, leading Amazon to success.

Balancing Flexibility and Innovation

Yi Sun-sin's leadership exemplifies the harmony of flexibility and innovation, achieving success even under challenging conditions. By adapting his strategies, utilizing resources efficiently, and building strong relationships with his team, he provided a valuable model for leadership in turbulent times.

Today's leaders must navigate changing markets with flexible strategies, maximize resources, and build strong relationships to achieve success. Yi Sun-sin's leadership transcends his era, underscoring the necessity of balancing innovation and flexibility.

Chapter 2: Future-Oriented Management

2.1 The Importance of Long-Term Vision and Strategic Planning: Lessons from *The Romance of The Three Kingdoms* and Admiral Yi Sun-sin

For leaders, envisioning the future and developing long-term plans are critical elements that influence organizational success. Both Liu Bei from *The Romance of The Three Kingdoms* and Admiral Yi Sun-sin were leaders who held long-term visions, focusing steadily on their ultimate goals rather than being driven solely by short-term gains. Their examples offer valuable lessons to modern leaders on the importance of planning and preparing for the future.

Liu Bei's Long-Term Vision: A Steady Pursuit Toward Unification of *The Three Kingdoms*

In *The Romance of The Three Kingdoms*, Liu Bei pursued the long-term goal of unifying *The Three Kingdoms*, expanding his influence steadily over time. Though he faced numerous defeats and setbacks, Liu Bei's leadership demonstrated the importance of pursuing long-term goals with patience and resilience, without being swayed by immediate success.

Instead of seeking quick victories against powerful rivals

like Cao Cao and Sun Quan, Liu Bei focused on building and strengthening his forces over time. He prioritized placing talented individuals in key positions and dedicated significant effort to consolidating unity within his ranks. This approach characterized him as a leader with a forward-looking vision who was committed to long-term success rather than immediate gains.

A key aspect of Liu Bei's strategy was his consistent evaluation of his position and surroundings to anticipate future opportunities. Although he experienced military defeats, he used them as opportunities to rebuild and eventually establish the Kingdom of Shu-Han. His persistence and patience are indicative of the qualities necessary in a leader with a long-term vision.

In modern management, long-term vision and goal setting are equally essential. Focusing solely on short-term gains makes it difficult for organizations to achieve sustainable success.

For instance, Apple's founder, Steve Jobs, always maintained a long-term vision for product development. He saw each product not merely as a revenue source but as a crucial part of Apple's future vision. During the development of the iPhone, Jobs focused on the user experience and the Apple ecosystem, which ultimately led to the company's dominant position in the smartphone market.

The lesson from Liu Bei's leadership is clear: true leaders

should avoid being narrowly focused on short-term success and instead design concrete, long-term visions that guide their organizations toward sustained success.

Liu Bei spent years planning, securing talent, and strengthening internal unity to build a solid foundation for his ultimate goal of unifying *The Three Kingdoms*. Similarly, modern leaders must set a long-term vision and lead their organizations toward success through consistent efforts.

Admiral Yi Sun-sin's Long-Term Vision: A Mission to Protect the Nation

Admiral Yi Sun-sin also held a long-term vision centered on his mission to protect the nation. Rather than focusing on individual battle victories, he developed and executed strategies to ensure the long-term security of his country.

This long-term approach to national security was similar to Liu Bei's approach. Both leaders looked beyond immediate results and focused on the broader objective of ensuring their nations' futures.

During the Japanese invasions of Korea, Admiral Yi's innovations, such as the creation of the Turtle Ship, contributed to significant victories, but his true leadership lay in his ability to make decisions that secured his country's future. He wasn't satisfied with a single victory; instead, he analyzed the overall course of the war and sought the best ways to protect his country.

Admiral Yi's strategic approach offers today's leaders an important lesson: it is essential to make decisions with a long-term perspective rather than being overly focused on short-term results.

Leaders need to consider market changes and future uncertainties, develop long-term strategies, allocate resources accordingly, and provide stability to their organizations. Focusing solely on short-term profits can hinder long-term success—a lesson well illustrated by Admiral Yi's example.

In modern management, leaders must maintain a long-term perspective even amidst constant change and prepare their organizations for the future. For example, Amazon's Jeff Bezos had a long-term vision for Amazon from the early days when it was just an online bookstore. He aimed beyond book sales, focusing on global expansion through e-commerce and extending into future businesses like cloud services. Bezos's long-term vision was pivotal in transforming Amazon into a global powerhouse.

Leaders with a long-term vision, like Admiral Yi, are resilient to short-term setbacks and steadily advance toward their ultimate goals.

A leader's sense of mission is critical to an organization's long-term success, and it is essential to continually assess and refine plans to realize that mission.

Lessons from Long-Term Vision in Modern Management

The examples of Liu Bei from *The Romance of The Three Kingdoms* and Admiral Yi Sun-sin underscore the importance of having a long-term vision and preparing for the future. By setting long-term goals and pursuing them diligently, rather than fixating on immediate results, their leadership demonstrates the importance of long-term planning for organizational success.

Modern leaders should also prepare for their organizations' futures with a long-term perspective. By anticipating market changes, technological advancements, and political instability, and developing strategies that account for these factors, leaders can achieve sustainable growth. Additionally, leaders must share their vision with organizational members, ensuring consistent pursuit of common goals.

The leadership of Liu Bei and Admiral Yi Sun-sin emphasizes that long-term planning and vision are more important than immediate success. Leaders must set future-oriented goals for their organizations and work toward them consistently. By doing so, organizations can continue to grow in dynamic environments and maintain a strong competitive edge.

Chapter 3: The Attitude of a Future-Prepared Leader: Trend Forecasting and Innovation

Future-oriented management means not only addressing present challenges but also preparing to adapt to evolving environments from a long-term perspective.

Today's business environment is constantly shaped by various factors: rapid technological advances, economic uncertainties, political shifts, and social trends. Within this dynamic context, leaders must anticipate the future, preparing their organizations for sustained success and growth by strategizing for long-term outcomes.

For leaders to be future-ready, it is not enough to merely predict trends—they must deeply analyze them and develop innovative strategies that allow them to navigate and even lead these changes. They also need the ability to identify opportunities amid uncertainties and to capitalize on them.

Forecasting Future Trends: Reading the Direction of Change

Trend forecasting is an essential skill for leaders. By sensing market changes early and creating strategies accordingly, organizations can maintain a competitive edge in an ever-shifting environment.

Especially in modern society, where technological and social changes are accelerating, accurately forecasting future trends and preparing accordingly can be critical to organizational success.

Disney, for example, evolved from a traditional film and TV content company to meet changing media consumption trends with its streaming service, Disney+. Recognizing the shift toward digital platforms and anticipating consumer needs, Disney created a foundation to compete against industry leaders like Netflix. With a massive content library and a powerful brand, Disney quickly established a strong foothold in the streaming market.

Similarly, Howard Schultz, CEO of Starbucks, foresaw shifts in consumer coffee culture and lifestyle, reshaping the café industry with a long-term strategy.

Schultz transformed Starbucks from a mere coffee vendor into a "third place" for people to relax, work, and socialize. By creating a cultural space, Starbucks differentiated itself from conventional cafés and established a unique position globally. The company also implemented digital services, including mobile ordering and a digital rewards system, and adjusted swiftly to the COVID-19 pandemic with non-contact services, ensuring sustainable growth in changing environments.

By combining convenience with a unique digital experience, Starbucks set itself apart from other coffee chains. These examples show how leaders who forecast trends and innovate business models create enduring competitive advantages.

To accurately forecast future trends and prepare for success, leaders must thoroughly understand market dynamics and consumer behavior. In addition, they must assess how external factors—such as technological advancements and policy changes—affect their industry.

These capabilities are vital for developing long-term growth strategies.

Ensuring Sustainability Through Innovation

One of the most effective ways to adapt to future changes is through innovation. Innovation encompasses not only new product development but also reimagining existing business models to create new value. Innovative thinking and strategy allow organizations to stay competitive and promote sustainable growth in changing environments.

Procter & Gamble (P&G) exemplifies how innovative strategies can drive organizational sustainability. To differentiate itself in a competitive market, P&G consistently invests in product innovation.

By predicting consumer preferences and launching environmentally-friendly products, P&G has stayed relevant in the consumer goods market. For example, P&G has introduced eco-friendly products and smart home appliances, integrating technology with product development. This commitment to innovation has helped P&G remain a global leader.

Likewise, General Electric (GE) has shifted from traditional manufacturing toward an innovative business model that combines industrial expertise with cutting-edge technology. By employing digital twin technology, GE has optimized asset management and manufacturing processes, opening new markets with technology-driven solutions.

GE's case illustrates how innovation—by moving beyond traditional approaches—can help an organization achieve sustainability and thrive in a rapidly evolving industry.

Innovation is not only a crucial strategy for adapting to future changes but also a key element for leadership that actively guides those changes. Leaders must use innovative thinking to identify new opportunities and transform them into sustainable growth through strategic leadership.

Digital Transformation and Preparing for the Future

Digital transformation is another strategic imperative for future-focused leaders. This involves leveraging digital tools and data to modernize every aspect of an organization's processes and services, maximizing efficiency, and creating new business models. In today's fast-evolving technological environment, digitalization provides a critical opportunity to align organizations with a digital-first strategy.

Major financial institutions, such as HSBC, have embraced digital transformation to prepare for the future. HSBC has invested in strengthening its digital banking system and partnered with fintech startups to improve customer service.

Digital banking and online financial services enhance customer experience, reduce operational costs, and improve resource management efficiency. HSBC's digital transformation shows how traditional industries can remain competitive and prepare for future changes by embracing digitalization.

Siemens in Germany also successfully implemented digital transformation through an industrial IoT platform, creating smart factories. Siemens optimized manufacturing processes by integrating data for real-time analysis, reducing costs and improving quality. Siemens's case demonstrates how digitalization can ensure future competitiveness in manufacturing and how leaders can strengthen organizational sustainability through digital transformation.

To succeed in digital transformation, it is crucial to harness advanced technologies such as data analytics, automation, and artificial intelligence (AI). These technologies improve efficiency, reduce costs, and enhance customer experience.

Leaders must utilize digital transformation to innovatively improve every process within their organizations, building future-ready business models.

Leadership and Change Management for Future Preparedness

To prepare for the future, leaders must embody transformational leadership, guiding organizations through necessary changes. This involves overcoming resistance to change within the organization and creating an environment where members can embrace change positively. Leaders must understand the importance of change management and proactively work to innovate organizational culture and structure.

British airline EasyJet is an example of a company that led industry transformation through digital transformation. EasyJet introduced automation and digital systems to optimize aircraft maintenance and passenger booking processes. This enhanced operational efficiency and simultaneously reduced costs and improved service quality by leveraging data and technology.

In contrast, Kodak's failure illustrates the fate of companies unable to adapt to change. Despite anticipating the rise of digital cameras, Kodak clung to its traditional film business and resisted transformation, leading to its inability to compete in the digital age. Kodak's case serves as a cautionary tale that if leaders fail to drive change or adapt to future trends, companies risk rapid obsolescence.

ESG Management for Sustainability
Another critical aspect of future-focused management is ESG (environmental, social, and governance) management.

ESG represents responsible management that incorporates environmental, social, and governance factors, now essential for ensuring an organization's long-term sustainability.

Daimler has transformed from a traditional car manufacturer to a company focused on electric vehicles and sustainable energy usage. By investing in electric vehicles and renewable energy, Daimler is leading an environmentally-friendly automotive industry, reducing carbon emissions, and promoting sustainable energy use.

ESG management plays a pivotal role not only in enhancing a company's image but also in securing long-term sustainability by fulfilling social responsibilities. Environmentally responsible companies contribute to addressing climate change and resource depletion, while socially responsible companies build trust through fair business practices and strong relationships with employees, consumers, and communities.

Transparent governance strengthens investor and shareholder trust, ensuring long-term growth and stability.

Ultimately, leaders need a future-focused mindset characterized by innovative thinking and a long-term vision. By driving digital transformation, embracing ESG management, and leading change, leaders can maintain sustainability and competitiveness in changing environments.

A leader's readiness for the future goes beyond merely anticipating trends; it involves taking charge of these shifts and demonstrating strategic leadership that aims for long-term success.

Part 6: The Path to Sustainable Growth and New Challenges

The leadership lessons and strategies presented in this book, drawn from the lives of heroes in *The Three Kingdoms* and General Yi Sun-sin, illustrate the qualities and strategic thinking that today's leaders can study and apply.

Each of these figures demonstrated the ability to adapt to constantly changing environments as leaders, displaying strong decision-making skills and a sense of responsibility even in the midst of crises.

Their stories offer valuable principles of leadership that provide modern leaders with opportunities for self-growth and professional development.

Vision and Goal-Setting

Through the examples of Liu Bei and General Yi Sun-sin, we emphasized that long-term vision is crucial for guiding an organization's direction, while setting clear goals is an essential skill for leaders. A leader should look beyond short-term gains, holding a far-reaching vision to prepare the organization for the future.

Importance of Talent Management and Communication

The examples of Zhuge Liang and General Yi Sun-sin's management of subordinates highlight the importance of placing the right people in the right roles and building trust through communication, both of which are vital for an organization's success. Leaders should foster a trust-based environment with team members, maximizing organizational performance through effective communication.

Crisis Management and Decision-Making

In the chapters on crisis management and decisiveness, the cases of the Battle of Red Cliffs and the Battle of Myeongnyang illustrated the importance of the decisiveness and responsibility leaders must exhibit in times of crisis. By making swift and confident decisions and taking responsibility for the outcomes, leaders can earn their organization's trust.

Learning from Failure

Through the setbacks and comebacks of Liu Bei and General Yi Sun-sin, we explored how essential it is for leaders to view failure as an opportunity for growth rather than a setback. Failure provides new insights, enabling leaders to develop stronger strategies for the future.

Forward-Looking Management

Finally, we examined how Sun Quan's and General Yi Sun-sin's adaptable leadership styles demonstrate the importance of anticipating changes in markets and technology trends. Leaders must predict future shifts and pursue sustainable growth through innovative strategies.

Core Elements of Leadership

Across all chapters, the main point emphasized is that the essence of leadership lies in adapting to change, learning from failure, and sustaining a long-term vision. Leaders have a responsibility that goes beyond managing outcomes: they must prepare for the future, while also creating an environment that maximizes their teams' potential.

Sustainable Growth and Self-Development as a Leader

The path of a leader is never a completed journey. It is an endless road of constant change, new challenges, and, at times, inevitable failures. Like the historical figures introduced in this book, leaders must commit to continuous learning and growth. Their successes were not born from natural genius or flawless plans, but rather through a process of deriving lessons from failures and consistently developing themselves.

Self-development is a vital element of leadership. Leaders are required to stay informed about new technologies and trends, anticipate shifts in the market, and continuously expand their knowledge. This learning process goes beyond books or formal education; it is achieved through real-world experience and regular self-reflection.

1. The Importance of Self-Reflection and Feedback
Successful leaders frequently review their actions and use feedback to improve. Leaders must understand their strengths and weaknesses, engage in ongoing learning and self-reflection to address those gaps, and treat failures and mistakes as opportunities for growth. Cultivating an openness to others' perspectives is equally crucial.

2. Networking and Collaboration
Leaders are expected to learn and collaborate through networks with other leaders. Especially when connecting with leaders within the same industry, these interactions provide valuable opportunities to gain fresh ideas and perspectives. Recognizing the importance of collaboration and maximizing strengths through partnerships are indispensable qualities for successful leaders.

3. Embracing Challenges
Successful leaders do not shy away from challenges but instead embrace them as opportunities for growth. Like the heroes of *The Three Kingdoms* and General Yi Sun-sin, the ability to turn crises into opportunities is a core aspect of leadership. Change and uncertainty are ever-present on a leader's journey, and it is essential to embrace these actively and face challenges head-on.

4. Ongoing Learning in Technology and Trends
Today's business environment is constantly being redefined by rapidly evolving technologies. AI, data analytics, and digital transformation are essential elements that leaders must understand and apply. Leaders of the future must respond quickly to technological shifts and continuously learn to seize new opportunities.

Continue Learning and Embrace Challenges to the End

The final message of this book is that the path of a leader is never a simple, straightforward journey towards a stable goal. Leaders have the role of finding new opportunities amidst constant challenges and change, deriving lessons from failures, and driving sustainable growth for both themselves and their organizations.

The heroes of *The Three Kingdoms* and General Yi Sun-sin displayed powerful leadership in times of crisis, persevering steadfastly towards their goals. Their stories provide strong inspiration for modern leaders to grow through continuous learning and embracing challenges.

To Our Readers

We hope that this book has provided you with meaningful insights into the journey of leadership.

The stories of the figures in *The Three Kingdoms* and General Yi Sun-sin extend beyond historical events, offering the wisdom and courage needed in the critical moments and choices that modern leaders face. Each of these figures found their own path amidst different historical and environmental contexts, showing true leadership qualities and achieving timeless greatness. The path you walk in leadership will not differ greatly from theirs.

Leadership is more than simply guiding an organization; it is a continuous process of self-growth and presenting a brighter future for both the organization and society.

With the hope that the lessons presented in this book will serve you on your journey, here are four key points to remember as you move forward:

1. Adapt Flexibly to Change

Change is an unavoidable reality, constantly present before us. In *The Three Kingdoms*, Sun Quan was able to sustain his power for a long time by adapting between collaboration and rivalry with Cao Cao and Liu Bei, thanks to his adaptability.

Similarly, General Yi Sun-sin succeeded in unfavorable conditions on the battlefield by adapting swiftly with flexible tactics. Their stories offer critical lessons on how leaders should respond flexibly in changing environments.

The modern business environment is no different. With technological advances, market fluctuations, and shifting consumer expectations, new challenges constantly confront us. Yet, it is precisely these adaptable leaders who can steer organizations steadily and create opportunities for growth.

Change can sometimes evoke fear and cause us to lose our way amidst uncertainty. However, leaders are those who find opportunities within such change and connect them to organizational success. Do not avoid change; embrace it. Change is a door that opens new possibilities for organizational growth.

Leaders must consistently recalibrate themselves, transforming their vision into reality amid uncertainty, and finding new paths within those changes.

The changes your organization faces may initially appear to be crises. However, they are also new opportunities. By adapting flexibly to change, your leadership will shine even brighter.

Change is a constant companion in a leader's life. At times, change may bring fear and doubt. However, a leader is one who overcomes such moments and finds ways to adapt to change.

Recognize opportunities within the new environments brought by change, and use these to build a foundation for organizational growth. When you are a leader who adapts flexibly to change, you will always be able to move forward.

2. Do Not Fear Failure

Failure is something that comes to everyone, but how we accept it can greatly alter its meaning.

In *The Three Kingdoms*, Liu Bei experienced multiple defeats and was forced to live as a fugitive for a long time. He encountered many hardships—losing battles, being betrayed by allies, and even losing his own army. However, rather than succumb to these failures, Liu Bei overcame them and ultimately achieved his dream as Emperor of Shu-Han. His failures did not end in defeat but instead became a driving force that led him to develop better strategies, forge new alliances, and rebuild his army.

Similarly, General Yi Sun-sin faced unjust setbacks due to political conspiracies and demotions. His time in prison may have been a moment of deep personal despair. Nevertheless, he did not yield to the situation. Instead, he took the opportunity to reflect on himself and prepare for the future. When the critical moment came to defend his homeland, he returned to the battlefield and achieved victory. Failure only made him stronger, and his decisions and leadership on the battlefield shone even more brightly as a result.

As leaders, you too will experience failures. You may feel frustrated when plans don't go as expected or when unforeseen issues arise. However, what truly matters is what you learn from those failures and how you rise again. Failure is not merely an end; it is part of the process of moving toward a better future.

Do not fear failure. Instead, view it as an opportunity to learn and grow.

Failure comes to everyone, but how you respond will determine the growth of your leadership. Failure is a stepping stone to new success and an essential process for deepening and strengthening your experience. Embrace failure without fear, and carve out new paths within it.

3. Commit to Constant Learning and Growth

When I took the role of CEO, someone gave me a book with the words, "The answers are in books." Since then, this message has stayed with me, becoming a guiding principle in my approach to management. The wisdom and lessons I've gained from books have deeply influenced my management philosophy and served as an essential compass in overcoming various challenges and crises.

Leadership is a never-ending process of learning. Zhuge Liang achieved many victories through his exceptional wisdom but never lost his commitment to continuous learning and growth. He immersed himself in study and knowledge, continually developing his leadership skills.

Likewise, General Yi Sun-sin pursued learning even during the war, constantly researching new strategies and tactics, walking a never-ending path of learning. Their leadership was not merely a product of natural genius; it was based on the wisdom gained through relentless study.

In modern business, successful leaders must also recognize the importance of learning. Technology evolves daily, and market conditions change rapidly.

No matter how much you have achieved, don't remain stagnant. Continuous learning and growth will lead to the growth of your organization as well. Leaders are those who always seek to learn something new and guide their organization in a better direction based on what they learn.

Learning is one of a leader's most valuable assets. Gaining new insights from various fields will allow you to see the world with a broad perspective.

As Steve Jobs sparked innovation by blending technology and the arts, you too can gather learnings from various fields to inspire fresh ideas and gain new inspiration.

A leader is someone who never stops learning.
When learning ceases, so does leadership. You must constantly continue developing yourself.

Learn new technologies, understand market trends, and gain broad insights through diverse experiences.
The wisdom you acquire through learning will make your leadership even more resilient.

4. Embrace Challenges

Leadership shines brightest when faced with challenges. Liu Bei endured numerous defeats but never abandoned his dream of unifying *The Three Kingdoms*, and General Yi Sun-sin, even when faced with overwhelming military forces, never retreated but stood resolute in battle.

They did not fear challenges and continued on their paths. It is precisely in times of challenge that leadership reveals its true value, turning the crises you encounter into new opportunities.

In the business environment you will face, there will undoubtedly be many challenges and obstacles. In those moments, as leaders, you will stand at pivotal crossroads that demand important decisions. Do not retreat in the face of challenges; forging new paths is the role of a leader.

Challenges are also a process that encourages leaders to discover new capabilities and fosters even greater growth.

While challenges may appear to be crises, they are also opportunities.

Do not shy away from challenges. Only leaders who trust themselves and move forward in the face of challenges can achieve true growth. The challenges you confront will make your leadership shine even brighter.

A leader is not someone who fears challenges, but rather one who demonstrates their capabilities through them.
Don't miss the opportunities within the challenges you face. Challenges are the key that can unlock even greater achievements and potential for you.

In Conclusion

I hope that through this book, you have been able to find direction for your growth as a leader.

The stories of Romance of *The Three Kingdoms* and General Yi Sun-sin embody timeless leadership principles that continue to resonate today. Each of these figures found their own path within challenging environments and, in doing so, demonstrated crucial principles of leadership.

I hope that these lessons will prove useful in your own journey of leadership. Keep learning, and keep challenging yourself. Your leadership will play an essential role in building a better future for your organization and society.

On this journey of learning and challenge, endless possibilities await you.

On a beautiful day in October 2024

www.ingramcontent.com/pod-product-compliance
Lightning Source LLC
Chambersburg PA
CBHW071501220526
45472CB00003B/879